THERE IS NO
SUCH THING AS A
"CRACK HEAD" OR
A "DOPE FIEND"

The
Miseducation
of America

DR. DEBORAH DAY AIKENS

PABLO ESCOBAR | SCARFACE | PHARMACEUTICAL COMPANIES:
THE FIRST ONE IS ALWAYS FREE!

outskirtspress
DENVER, COLORADO

Acknowledgments

With grace and humility, I pay homage to my Higher Power from which all things are possible.

To the memory of my grandfather, Frederick C. Ferguson, who empowered me with the light of knowledge.

To my parents and grandparents, who instilled in me a sense of security and perseverance.

To my spiritual soul mate: my best friend, my husband, and to our children who remind me everyday, just how blessed I am.

To all of the sick and suffering addicts: Remember the passage: "I once was lost but now am found." (Amazing Grace)

Remember you are God's child.

Concepts

Crack head:
A derogatory term used to denote someone who is addicted to crack cocaine.

Dope fiend:
A derogatory term used to denote someone who is addicted to heroin.

Individuals who refer to others as crack head and dope fiend:
Misinformed, naive, or ignorant

If you fall anywhere within the last category which many Americans do, please read on. Open your eyes and see: Open your ears and listen: Open your mind and be enlightened.

The magnitude of the names identified in the following book speaks to the reality of how pervasive drugs are in America. All names and their affiliation with any drug is a matter of public record.

Table of Contents

SPIRIT

WHITNEY HOUSTON

August 9, 1963-February 11, 2012

Alcohol, Marijuana, Cocaine, Prescription Drug History

SPIRIT

MICHAEL JACKSON

August 29, 1958-June 25, 2009

Propofol, Lorazepam, Midazolam

SPIRIT

JAMES BROWN

"God Father of Soul"

May 3, 1933-December 25, 2006

Prescription Pain Killers

&

Other Alcohol & Drug History

SPIRIT

ELVIS PRESLEY

January 8, 1935-August 16, 1977

Prescription Drugs History

SPIRIT

JIMI HENDRIX

November 27, 1942-September 18, 1970

Alcohol, Sleeping Pills, Psychedelic Drugs

SPIRIT

MARILYN MONROE

June 1, 1926-August 5, 1962

Barbiturates

LOST SOULS

Do you know these musicians who died from a drug overdose or who had a drug history?

Adam Golstein (DJ AM)
March 30, 1973-August 28, 2009
Cocaine, Oxycodone, Vicodin, Ativan,
Klonopin, Xanax, Benadryl, Levamisole

Gerald Levert
July 13, 1966-November 10, 2006
Vicodin, Percocet, Darvocet,
Xanax, Antihistimines

Pimp C
December 29, 1973-December 4, 2007
Promethazine and Codeine "Sizzurp"

Ol' Dirty Bastard
November 15, 1968-November 13, 2004
Cocaine & Tramadol

Ike Turner
November 5, 1931-December 12, 2007
Cocaine

D J Screw
July 20, 1971-November 16, 2000
Lethal Dose of Codeine & Other Drugs

Kevin Mark DuBrow
(Lead Vocalist for Quiet Riot)
October 29, 1955-November 19, 2007
Cocaine

Rob Pilatus (Milli Vanilli)
June 8, 1965-April 2, 1998
Alcohol and Prescription Drugs

Notorious B.I.G.
May 21, 1972-March 9, 1997
Prescription Drugs

Stephen Maynard Clark (Def Leppard)
April 23, 1960-June 8, 1991
Codeine, Valium, Morphine, Alcohol

Phyllis Hyman
July 6, 1949-June 30, 1995
Barbiturates

Keith Moon (the Who)
August 23, 1946-September 7, 1978
Prescription Sedatives

LOST SOULS

Kristen Pfaff
(Bass Guitarist: Hole)
May 26, 1967-June 16, 1994
Heroin

Janis Joplin
January 19, 1943-October 4, 1970
Heroin

David Ruffin
January 18, 1941-June 1, 1991
Cocaine

Frankie Lymon
September 30, 1942-February 27, 1968
Heroin

Brian Epstein (Beatles Manager)
September 19, 1934-August 27, 1967
Barbiturates

Tommy Dorsey
November 19, 1905-November 26, 1956
Complication from Sedatives

John Coltrane
September 23, 1926-July 17, 1967
Heroin

Charlie "Bird" Parker
August 29, 1920-March 12, 1955
Heroin & Alcohol

Dinah Washington
August 29, 1924-December 14, 1963
Barbiturates

Miles Davis
May 25, 1926-September 28, 1991
History of Cocaine and Heroin

Billie Holiday
April 7, 1915-July 17, 1959
Complications from Narcotics &
Alcohol

Note: The "27 Club," is an interesting phenomena of famous musicians who died at the age of 27: They include Brian Jones, Jimi Hendrix, Janis Joplin, Jim Morrison and Kurt Cobain just to name a few. According to Wikipedia, "The impetus for the club's creation were the deaths of seemingly unusual number of prominent 27-year-old musicians within a two-year period of time." And as time passed, we have lost Amy Winehouse: Dead at 27!

LOST SOULS

Do you know of these actors who died from a
drug overdose or who had a drug history?

Billy Mays (Oxy Clean Man)
July 20, 1958 – June 28, 2009
Cocaine found in bloodstream

Karen Lancaume (Baise-moi)
January 19, 1973-January 28, 2005
Temazepam

Brittany Murphy
November 10, 1977-December 20, 2009
Multiple Drug Intoxication (Accidental)

Trevor Goddard
(Mortal Kombat, JAG)
October 14, 1962-June 7, 2003
Heroin, Cocaine, Temazepam, Vicodin

Heath Ledger
April 4, 1979-January 22, 2008
Prescription Drugs

Elisa Bridges (Playboy Playmate)
May 24, 1973-February 7, 2002)
Acute Intoxication Heroin,
Methamphetamines, Meperidine, and
Alprazolam

Brad Renfro
July 25, 1982-January 15, 2008
Heroin / Morphine Intoxication

Catya "Cat" Sassoon
September 3, 1968-January 1, 2002
Hydromorphone and Cocaine

Anna Nicole Smith
(Model-Sex Symbol)
November 28, 1967-February 8, 2007
Prescription Drugs

Anissa Jones (Family Affair)
March 11, 1958-August 28, 1976
Cocaine, PCP, Quaaludes, Seconal

Dana Plato (Different Strokes)
November 7, 1963-May 8, 1999
Soma and Vicodin

George Sanders
(The Ghost and Mrs. Muir)
July 3, 1906-April 25, 1972
Nembutal

LOST SOULS

River Phoenix
August 23, 1970-October 31, 1993
Heroin and Cocaine (Speedball)

Pier Angeli
June 19, 1932-September 10, 1971
Barbiturate Overdose

Linda Wong (Adult Films)
September 13, 1951-December 17, 1987
Xanax, Cloral-Hydrate, Alcohol

Inger Stevens
October 18, 1934-April 30, 1970
Pharmaceuticals and Alcohol

Judy Garland
June 10, 1922-June 22, 1969
Barbiturates (Accidental)
Cirrhosis of the Liver, (not the cause of death)

Robert Pastorelli (Murphy Brown)
"Acute Cocaine-Morphine(Heroin) toxicity"

Scotty Beckett (Our Gang)
October 4, 1929-May 10, 1968
Barbiturates or Alcohol

Wallace Reid
(Silent Films, "The Screen's Most Perfect Lover")
April 15, 1891-January 18, 1923
Morphine History

Dorothy Dandridge
November 9, 1922-September 8, 1965
Pharmaceuticals (Accidental overdose)

LOST SOULS

Do you know these comedians who died from a
drug overdose or who had a drug history?

Lenny Bruce
October 13, 1925–August 3, 1966
"Acute Morphine Poisoning"

Chris Farley (Saturday Night Live)
February 15, 1964–December 18, 1997
Cocaine and Morphine

John Belushi
(Saturday Night Live)
January 24, 1949–March 5, 1982
Cocaine and Heroin (Speedball)

Richard Pryor
Comedian/Actor
December 1, 1940–December 10, 2005
Freebase and Alcohol History (Unrelated
to death)

LOST SOULS

Do you know these athletes who died from a
drug overdose or who had a drug history?

Eric Show (Pitcher)
September 1, 1961-January 19, 2007
Cocaine and Anti-Anxiety Drugs

Ken Caminiti (Baseball-MVP)
April 21, 1963-October 10, 2004)
Cocaine and Opiates (Speedball)

Bam Bam Bigelow (Wrestler)
May 19, 1956-March 16, 1994
Cocaine and Heroin (Speedball)

Len Bias (Basketball)
November 18, 1963-June 19, 1986
Cocaine

Brian Adams (Wrestler)
January 31, 1963-August 13, 2007
Painkillers and Illegal Steroid Related

Eddie Guerrero (Wrestler)
October 9, 1967-November 13, 2005
Alcohol and Painkiller History
(Unrelated to death)

"YET's": Jails, Institutions, Death, or Recovery?

"YET's" (You're Eligible Too): Jails, Institutions, Death or Recovery: Which will it be? The following are people you know, or people you know of, who have struggled with addiction, and may or may not be currently using; or who are currently active drug abusers.

Rush Limbaugh- painkillers
Bobby Brown- alcohol, cocaine, marijuana
Lindsey Lohan- alcohol, cocaine
Courtney Love-heroin, oxicodone
Yasmine Bleeth-cocaine, methamphetamines
El DeBarge-crack cocaine
Brittany Spears-alcohol
Paris Hilton-marijuanna & cocaine
Corey Feldman-heroin
Robert Downey Jr.-alcohol, cocaine, heroin, valium
Johnny Depp-alcohol and some drugs
Collin Farrell-cocaine, alcohol
Tim Allen-cocaine
McKenzie Phillips-cocaine, meth, alcohol, ecstasy
David Hasselhoff-alcohol
Mel Gibson-alcohol
Richard Dreyfuss-alcohol and other drugs

Winona Ryder-prescription drugs
DMX- dextromethorphan cough medicine
Keith Richards-heroin, alcohol
Flava Flave-crack
Bridget Nielson-alcohol
Josh Hamilton-crack cocaine
Nikki Sixx-heroin
Eric Clapton-heroin
David Bowie-cocaine, marijuana
Eddie Van Halen-alcohol, cocaine, methamphetamines
Tommy Lee-opiates, cocaine, alcohol
Eddie Money-oxycontin, alcohol
Boy George-cocaine
Judy Carne-marijuana, heroin
Robin Williams-alcohol, cocaine
Mel Griffith-alcohol and other drugs
Mathew Perry-vicodin and other prescription drugs
Jason Priestley-alcohol
Mickey Rourke-alcohol and drugs, GHB

Macaulay Culkin-???
Todd Bridges-drugs
Dennis Rodman-alcohol
Eminem-sleep drugs
Nicole Richie-alcohol, heroin,
    marijuana, vicodin
Charlie Sheen-alcohol, cocaine
Gary Busey-alcohol, cocaine
Kid Rock-alcohol
Lil Wayne-codeine
Snopp Dog-marijuana
Elton John-cocaine, alcohol
Ringo Star-alcohol, cocaine
Dione Warwick-marijuana
Liza Minnelli-cocaine, alcohol
Kem- drugs & alcohol
Demi Moore-alcohol, cocaine, nitris-
    oxide, synthetic marijuana? "She
    smoked something."
Stacy "Fergie" Ferguson-crystal-meth
Willy Nelson-marijuana and
    mushrooms
Ozzie Osborn-cocaine, alcohol
Billy Joel-alcohol
Samuel Jackson-cocaine, alcohol
Daniel Baldwin-prescription drugs
Chyna Doll- prescription drugs, alcohol
Jaimee Foxworth-alcohol, marijuana
Steven Adler-speedballs

Nick Nolte-alcohol, GHB
Tom Arnold-cocaine, alcohol, marijuana
Jessie James alcohol and other drugs
Drew Barrymore-alcohol, cocaine,
    marijuana
Melanie Griffith-alcohol and other drugs
Jamie Lee Curtis-morphine
Kirsty Alley-cocaine
Paula Abdul-prescription drugs
Tonya Harding-meth
Brett Favre-vicodin
Mike Tyson-cocaine
Darrell Strawberry-cocaine, alcohol
Lawrence Taylor-cocaine
Dwight Gooden-cocaine, alcohol
Jose Conseco-steroids
Heidi Fleiss-crystal meth, valium, xanax
Naomi Campbell-alcohol and other drugs
Kate Moss-cocaine
Bill Murray-alcohol and various drugs
Chevy Chase-painkillers, alcohol
Martin Lawrence-psychotropic drugs
Buzz Aldrin-alcohol
Steven Tyler-cocaine, prescription drugs

Note: This list is not inclusive of all the living people who have extensive drug histories. In addition, as of to date, some of these individuals are in recovery or are abstaining from drugs. Keep in mind, however, that there is no cure and no guarantees: Recovery is a life long process.

CHAPTER 1

Reflections of Those We Have Lost

America, we are faced with the inevitable destruction of our spirits and consequently mankind. As sure as global warming, genocide through drug abuse, drug addiction, and other addictive patterns will, as it is, be our inevitable down fall. Ironically, it is not the drug and the behavior which will be the weapon of mass destruction, but our ignorance which allows us to turn a blind eye and a deaf ear to the ultimate ramifications of our behavior. Our naivety, which allows us to minimize the problem, and our denial, which acts as a guard dog keeping watch over our addictions, enables them to survive; they are maniacally manifesting through drugs and all other self defeating, obsessive compulsive behaviors which mask an even more insidious "dis-ease" with self.

America, wake up and look around you, we are losing spirits that we love. Whitney, you are God's child. Michael we miss you. It's been a little more than three years and we mourn your loss but live through your spirit. James Brown, Jimmie Hendrix, Elvis Presley Marilyn Monroe: In the native tradition we speak your name and your spirits live. Musicians: Adam Goldstein, Pimp C, Ike Turner, Kevin Du Brow, Gerald Levert, Ol' Dirty Bastard, DJ Screw, Rob Pilatus, Notorious B.I.G., Phyllis Hyman, Kristen Pfaff, David Ruffin, Miles Davis, John Coltrane, Stephen Clark, Keith Moon, Janis Joplin, Frankie Lymon, Brian Epstein, Dinah Washington, Billie Holiday, Tommy Dorsey, Charlie "Bird" Parker; Actors: Wallace Reid, George Sanders, Judy Garland, Dorothy Dandridge, Scotty Beckett, Nick Adams,

Pier Angeli, Inger Stevens, Linda Wong, Robert Pastorelli, Anissa Jones, Paula Yates, Trevor Goddard, Dana Plato, Anna Nicole Smith, Cataya "Cat" Sassoon, River Phoenix, Brittney Murphy, Karen Lancaume, Elisa Bridges, Heath Ledger and Brad Renfro; Comedians: Lenny Bruce, John Belushi, Chris Farley and Richard Pryor; Athletes: Eric Show, Bam Bam Bigelow, Brian Adams, Ken Caminiti, Len Bias, and Eddie Guerrero: Your spirits live.

Who are all of these people who have lost their way: "crack heads," "dope fiends," I think not! They are lost souls who succumbed to the disease of addiction. We humbly pay homage to all of the sick and suffering souls whose pain and misery transcends life with the expectation of an existence filled with peace and serenity. We snapped our fingers and stomped our feet to the beat of their music, songs that moved us; that encouraged us to take a look at our souls; songs that gave us pride; and songs that were shaped and defined by the reality of our existence; that crossed generations and became one with all that is part of our universe. Actors and actresses- We tuned in and turned on to them; we stood on long lines and bought tickets to see them in living color. We loved them; we looked up to them with hope; we held on to every word; we jubilated their triumphs and we cried and were saddened by their loss. Models- We were captivated by your beauty and allured by your lifestyle and fantasized; "What if," as if your life was a standard by which we could all follow. Athletes- We cheered them on, holding our breath, waiting for the next goal, the next touchdown, the next score, and the next homerun! We laughed until we cried as our comedians entertained us, turning pain into pleasure, minimizing the sharp edges of reality. The arts: One of the few things that make us socially cohesive; that bring us together as we celebrate the gift of the human spirit. Such high expectations we had of them: Minimizing their transgressions; condemning them in one moment and exalting them in the next.

To Michael and all of the lost souls in whose foot prints we walk, and to all that will follow in his footsteps: "What if"-What if we had listened to what you weren't saying? What if we had not closed our eyes to the glaring reality of your pain behind the empty smiles and the shallow wall? What if we were not allured and comforted by an illusion of calm and security? What if you were allowed to truly be you, not only through your art but with every breath you took everyday.

Your pain, your torment, your death can be a vehicle of redemption, a powerful message, but it is not. We continue the insanity of our ignorance which perpetuates the problem. We must begin to develop a relationship with self, with our spirit. We must begin to think in a different way. It is right there in front of us, our own insanity, doing the same thing and expecting a different result. We must learn not to aggravate the problem and learn from our past.

The Definition of Insanity is Doing the Same Thing and Expecting a Different Result

Robert Downey Junior was convicted and sentenced to jail time but was allowed furloughs to make movies! Paris Hilton's incarceration added insult to injury as she made a mockery of her sentence! Paris Hilton served five days of a 45 day sentence for violating probation on a DUI Charge. This sentence follows: Driving While Under the Influence of Alcohol, a license suspension, a plea of No Contest to a reckless driving charge, driving with a suspended license and failure to enroll in a court ordered alcohol education program. Despite the severity of her history and her total disregard for the law, special allowances were made for her to be held away from the general population, in a special unit reserved for police officers, politicians, celebrities and other high profile offenders. Furthermore, her release was predicated on a "medical consideration" which legitimated her serving the remaining 40 days of her sentence in the sanctity of her own home with an ankle monitoring device. Subsequent marijuana possession in both South Africa and the French Island of Cursica would follow along with a plea deal for Felony Cocaine Possession.

Charlie Sheen was convicted. Although his charge was not directly drug related, he does have a history of addiction and treatment and the nature of his angry, explosive behavior is symptomatic of the same pathology that drives his substance abuse. Despite the severity of his charge, he was able to delay sentencing because of his insistence on not being able to go to jail because of his nicotine addiction. His sentence was consequently amended to include working at a theatre in Aspen, and special allowances for him to smoke were made because of his smoking addiction! Charlie Sheen's addictive attitude continued to manifest itself in out of control escapades including $20,000 of cocaine, prostitution, and destruction of property.

Lindsay Lohan is finally held accountable for her irresponsible behavior resulting from her disease of addiction. She is sentenced to 90 days in jail for violating a DUI Probation followed by 90 days in rehabilitation; yet our justice system allowed her to take pharmaceutical medication to jail with her including adderall, a powerful amphetamine and stimulant used to treat ADHD, zoloff, which is an anti-depressant, dilaudid, an opiate base painkiller which was prescribed to her several months before following dental surgery, trazodone, a supposedly non addictive sedative, and nexium for acid reflux. The irony is that mandatory drug testing, a modality which is used to determine if the addict is remaining abstinent, continued to yield positive for amphetamines and opiates which is only natural because of the prescription medication. Subsequent failed stints in drug rehabilitation, drug test, assault charges, Felony Grand Theft charges and costly bails would follow.

We all watched as Amy Winehouse went from a beautiful spirited young woman to a mere shell, a ghost, a dead woman walking in less than one year. She now joins our lost souls.

We met Ted Williams, "The man with the golden voice," who went from family man and successful radio announcer, to deserter and panhandler. America cheered for his success. On the surface he was a miracle, but in the darkness of addiction, he continued to drink. With insight and encouragement from Dr. Phil, Ted Williams agreed to treatment, and then he disappeared. Where was "The man with the golden voice?" With two body guards he left treatment to fly to his girlfriend's treatment facility with promises of marriage!

America, we are missing the point! These individuals are sick and suffering addicts. Have we not learned anything from Heath Ledger, Brittany Murphy and all of the other lost souls who have died from addiction? We did the same thing with every one else. We turned a blind eye, a deaf ear; we made excuses for them; we lied for them; we enabled them, and we lost them. The Paris Hiltons, the Charlie Sheens, the Lindsay Lohans need help, they need treatment. Robert Downey Junior seems to be getting it on his own volition through no help from us. And still, we don't want to take his recovery for granted because recovery is hard work and a life long change in attitude. The special privileges that Paris Hilton received even after breaking the law on more than one occasion was a miscarriage of justice. Furthermore, her "medical condition" did not preclude her from driving illegally or attending the MTV Awards! How many times and in how many ways does one have to get the message out that one's life is unmanageable. What will be said when she mows someone down driving while under the influence. In addition, her status does not exempt her from the consequences of addiction. "There are no big I's and little you's." Charlie Sheen was crying out for help reeking violence and havoc. His nicotine addiction is just one aspect of his problem. The progressively life threatening behavior, the severity of medical complications and numerous failed treatment attempts are serious indicators that Charlie Sheen needed help. Lindsay Lohan should certainly be accountable for breaking the law, violating probation and putting other lives in jeopardy, but listen to this America. It was more important for her general well being and for others that she received treatment, be stabilized and then be incarcerated. I know it's a wild concept to some, but treatment trumps incarceration anytime. How are you going to address the reality that she is an addict, right here, right now? Allowing an addict to take prescription drugs into prison is ludicrous. Addictive thinking will encourage an addict to alter the prescribed medication and use it abusively, to get high! And why is she allowed to take an opiate drug months after a dental procedure. Opiate medication is designed for relief of pain following a procedure. If one continues to have pain for months following an oral procedure, there is a problem which requires medical intervention not opiate drugs. Lindsay was finally referred to treatment. America was perplexed when she left to get high. Don't be surprised, she's an addict; it's a process.

Amy Winehouse: We looked at her and said, "Wow, she really looks bad." She required an intervention but we minimized her pain and we lost her!

Ted Williams: His journey of recovery was just beginning. The more celebrity status he acquired, the more "media recovery," the more difficult it was for him to process his life changes. He, like all others are a work in progress. No one said that recovery was easy. By the way, where is Ted now? America, do you even care?

America, don't be bedazzled by celebrity status. The same consideration we give to "common folk," is the same that must be given to individuals of notoriety. There is no difference: Pain is pain and death is death. We're sorry Whitney. It was so much easier to blame Bobby, but that condemnation left us blind. Our obliviousness, our denial, our ignorance is inexcusable! We lost you, but you gained peace. America, reference the countless individuals we love and admire that are alive and have a history of addiction or who are actively using drugs and engaging in obsessions. Addictions permeate our society. It is as natural to use drugs and engage in other euphoric self defeating behaviors as it is to breath the oxygen that sustains our life. The comfortabillity of dysfunction, the normalcy of insanity, are the seeds of one's destruction.

America, it is now or never. One must be honest, open, and willing to change one's attitude as it relates to addiction and it starts with the disassociation of addicts into them and us: The "crack heads" the "dope fiends" and you. The countless souls who are lost along with those who walk among us share commonality in spirit and grace. We are all in some way interconnected. Our spirits bind us to a power greater than ourselves.

CHAPTER 2

Look in the Mirror: "Crack Head," "Dope Fiend" or Me?

So you thought the "crack heads" and the "dope fiends" were the problem? Ok: If you have not learned anything thus far, lets ship them all out to sea. Are you Ok now? No more problem with those "worthless addicts." We won't miss them. Hell, we don't even know them; that's right, "them" "others" not even worthy of a name. Now look to your right, then to your left; who's left? Now look in the mirror: WOWWWW! Scary, huh!

Who Is An Addict?

Addicts are not always so identifiable. We all have those stereotypical visions of what the addict looks like: A homeless heroin addict lurking in the shadows of alleys and abandoned buildings, strung out, scratching and nodding but never hitting the ground, or the crack addict crazed, in poor physical and mental condition, relentlessly on a mission to secure his/her next hit of the pipe, the unemployed pot head, "chilling," going nowhere fast or the "tripped out" acid head. And of course we can't forget the Bowery drunks. Our delusions as to who is the addict, is further perpetuated by the glamorization of certain drugs and how we tend to dichotomize drugs into good and bad. For example, powdered cocaine has always been associated with the affluent, glamorized by powerful professionals and celebrities hobnobbing on yachts and at private parties. In the 80's, heroin became "heroin sheik" and a whole new population of affluent patrons began sniffing heroin.

So America, think about it. Why is there status in sniffing coke, but if I smoke coke, I'm a "crack head?" And why, if I sniff heroin, it is "heroin sheik," but if I shoot dope, I am a "dope fiend?" "A drug is a drug is a drug," and an "addict is an addict." Wake up my beloved. Set aside all of those preconceived notions about the addict for just one minute. Now go back to the mirror. What do you see? Have you ever considered yourself as a possible addict? The scope of addiction has been limited to illicit drugs. Have you ever stopped to consider the seven million and counting Americans who are addicted to prescription medications which federal statistics reveal outweigh addiction to marijuana, cocaine, heroin and ecstasy combined? (The U.S. Drug Enforcement Administration)

According to NBC correspondent, Mark Potter, (July 5, 2009), "There is an epidemic of prescription drug abuse." He was referencing someone who overdosed on a combination of pain killers and sedatives while celebrating New Years Eve. In August, 2008, ABC News reported on a suburban teenager whom after being prescribed a prescription pain medication, progressed from percocet to oxycontin to a cheaper heroin. His addiction culminated in him stealing and writing fraudulent checks to support a $300-$400 a day habit.

Although not a prescription medication, another potentially fatal trend among youth is snorting crushed Tylenol PM mixed with heroin. As reported in the NY Daily News, "Cheese, as it is called, sells for as little as $2 a hit and delivers a euphoric high followed by drowsiness. To keep the high, users need to snort it up to 15 times a day" (Simone Weichselbaum, October 12, 2010.) Even more alarming is that the deadly combination is marketed to children in packets with cartoon characters and notable celebrities. Bonnie Miller brings light to another potentially dangerous trend in an article entitled, High on Cold and Cough Medicine. She relates, "It wasn't a street drug or a prescription painkiller that had nearly put Joe into a coma – her son had overdosed on ordinary cold medicine." (Good House Keeping October 5) It is interesting to note that the kids refer to the euphoria as "Robo Tripping." Miller references the Partnership for Drug Free America which relates, "One in eleven teenagers has gotten high on cold and cough medicine. The culprit is DXM-dextromethorphan, the cough suppressant ingredient in more than 140 cold remedies." Reportedly, "The medicine is inexpensive, legal and easy to find - large doses -a- package of tablets or a bottle of syrup - can produce the same euphoric and hallucinogenic effects as street drugs like pot or angel dust."

One should note the insanity of Joe's attitude. When asked if he was aware of the dangers of his actions he replied, "I know, but it's fun." Unfortunately, Joe's attitude extends to other potentially fatal practices by his adolescent counter parts. One may reference those notorious "pharm-parties," where children as young as twelve, shop in the family medicine cabinet, go to parties and empty all of their pills into a large glass container they call a fish bowl, and then proceed to grab a handful, calling it a trail mix, that they take with other narcotics and alcohol. These medications are also crushed and snorted giving them an instant and a more deadly high. Some how, however, we feel a little more secure when we can point the finger and project the problem on to someone else.

The extreme to which Americans will go, to alter their state of consciousness is reflected in a new trend which misuses bath salts. According to an article entitled, 'Bath Salts' Are Growing Drug Problem by Shelia Byrd (January, 2011) individuals are snorting, injecting, and smoking chemicals which are designed for bath salts. With alias such as Ivory Wave, Bliss, White Lightning, and Hurricane Charlie, the chemicals are more potent than the stimulant methamphetamine. They cause delirium, hallucinations and extreme violence. The travesty in this potentially deadly trend is not only that the chemicals are legal but in the reality that one would desire to engage in such extreme practices.

Speaking of new trends, one is reminded of America's sweetheart, Miley Cyrus, who decided to celebrate her eighteenth birthday by experimenting with a natural Mexican herb called Salvia. Identified as a "drug of concern" by the U.S. Drug Enforcement Agency, young people are allured by the drug's hallucinogenic effects. And what exactly was that substance Demi Moore was smoking? The reality that Americans believe that to truly have fun, one must get outside of one's self is alarming.

Drugs Are Not the Problem

We have been misinformed America. We have been led to believe that drugs are the problem. You know that all too familiar slogan, "The war on drugs." America may in fact spend hundreds of thousands on trying to eradicate drugs in America, but guess what? They never will because we want the drugs. It's Business 101: Supply and demand. So America: Ship all of the "dope fiends" and "crack addicts" out to sea: It's not going to solve the problem. Why? Well get ready for a real eye-opener. Drugs are not the problem, society is: our attitude, our insistence on getting high, or getting outside ourselves. What is more alarming is that we have become lulled in to a false sense that the problem lies within a designated population: Not my kind. America, it is not "them," it is "us." We have become desensitized to all of the disease that plagues our society. We look at each occurrence as an isolated phenomenon, thereby minimizing the complexity of the problem. In America there is an epidemic of addictive behaviors. Toohey relates that, "Some are addictive patterns while others are the seeds of a deep disease waiting to root into a poisonous plant that can kill us."

Pandemic of Addictive Behaviors and 12 Step Programs

It is important that we begin to look at addiction as a pandemic that potentially can rob the spirit of individuals and consequently, destroy culture as we know it. Consider just for a moment just some of the 12 Step Programs which exist:

Al-Anon/Alateen (1951)/(1957)
AA (Alcoholics Anonymous) (1935)
CA (Cocaine Anonymous (1982)
CLA (Clutters Anonymous) (1989)
CMA (Chrystal Meth Anonymous) (1994)
CoDa (Co-Dependents Anoymous) (1986
Co-Anon, for friends and families of addicts

COSA Codependents of Sex Addicts (1978)

COSLAA (CoSex and Love Addicts Anonymous)

DA (Debtors Anonymous) (1971) (1976)

EA (Emotions Anonymous) (1966) (1980)

EHA (Emotional Health Anonymous) (1971) (1973)

FA (Families Anonymous) (1971)

FA (Food Addicts in Recovery Anonymous) (1987) (Former member of OA)

FAA (Food Addicts Anonymous)

GA (Gamblers Anonymous) (1957)

GAM-Anon/Gam-A-Teen)

MA (Marijuana Anonymous) (1989)

NA (Narcotics Anonymous) (1953)

NAIL (Neurotics Anonymous) (1964)

Nar-Anon, for friends and family members of addicts (1971)

NicA (Nicotine Anonymous)(1982)

PA (Pills Anonymous) (1970's)

OA (Overeaters Anonymous) (1960)

OLGA (Online Gamblers Anonymous) (2002)

SA (Sexaholics Anonymous)(1979)

SAA (Sex Addicts Anonymous) (1977)

SCA (Sexual Compulsive Anonymous) (1982)

SA (Smokers Anonymous)

SLAA (Sex and Love Addicts Anonymous) (1976)

SIA (Survivors of Incest Anonymous) (1982)

WA (Workaholics Anonymous) (1983)

And we thought drugs were the problem!

Twelve Step Programs all follow, or are patterned after Alcoholics Anonymous which is based on a set of guiding principles for recovery from addictive and compulsive disorders. It supports the disease concept which eliminates any moral condemnation from one's addiction and places it within a medical and spiritual perspective. One is more than likely aware of AA and NA, however, there are at least six more recovery programs associated with drug addiction: CA, CMA, MA, NicA, PA, SA, for cocaine, crystal methamphetamine, marijuana, nicotine, and pills: By the way, nicotine and pills are drugs! In addition, there are four recovery programs for the family and significant others of addicts who are emeshed in dysfunctional relationships with the addict: CoDA, Co-Anon, FA, Nar-Anon. For individuals with eating disorders, there are FA, FAA, and OA. For individuals with sexual obsessions including lust, there are SA, SAA, SCA, and SLAA. In addition there are COSA and COSLAA for the codependents of sex addicts. For individuals who are obsessive clutters, there is CLA. For compulsive spenders there is DA, and for compulsive gamblers there are GA, and OLGA. For the friends and family members of problem gamblers there are Gam-Anon and Gam-A-Teen. For mental and emotional illnesses there are EA, EHA, and NAIL. Lastly, there is SIA for survivors of incest and WA for individuals who are compulsive workers including procrastinators and those who have an aversion to work.

The necessity of these 12 step programs translates to a very sick society of individuals who have become spiritually disconnected and who unguidedly seek satisfaction and gratification in substances and behaviors that gives them a false sense of security and control. Unfortunately, that immediate emotional gratification is really just an illusion of control.

The true understanding of addiction must be broadened. One's addiction to any behavior can not be minimized. The same attitude prevails. If you stop using the drugs for example, or you stop engaging in any addictive behavior and you do not work on the attitude of addiction then you are still an addict. The behavior is not as important as the attitude that perpetuates that behavior. That is why many addicts stop using their drug of choice only to end up transferring their obsession to another potentially addictive behavior. Countless times, I have heard a family member relic in the prospect that their significant other has 'overcome' their drug addiction, but on the other hand, they express grave concern because they have become abusive or they have become involved in maladaptive behavior that was not prevalent before. Once again, if you remove the substance and don't work on the attitude, the addiction prevails. All addictions are characterized by compulsive self defeating behavior. The psychic stimulation experienced by the drug addict is parallel to a similar experience by the gambler that wins a bet, the individual which finds serenity and solace in food, the shopper who makes an acquisition, etc. Again it is not the drug or the food or the purchase, it's the attitude behind the behavior - the feeling which is produced from the behavior.

Now for all of you skeptics: The chemical substances in the brain called neurotransmitters which are released when using drugs has a far more profound effect on the body; however, the reality is that those same substances are released when addicts indulge in all addictive behaviors. The release of adrenalin for example in runners is the same rush cocaine abusers achieve when they get high. The endorphins that are released that give the heroin addict a supreme feeling of euphoria, peace and well being are the same chemicals that are released when we are in pain.

The Internal State of Dis-ease: Personal Accounts

In America there is an epidemic of addictive behaviors. The stark reality is that America not only consumes 90% of the world's production of illicit drugs, we are addicted to food, sex, shopping, gambling, the Internet, pornography; the list is endless. Let's listen to some people you may know whose behavior you thought was quite normal who, in fact, were powerless over their addictions. In the following account, one smoker parallels her smoking to having a pimp:

One day the following question came to mind: What role does a pimp play or better yet, is it possible for a pimp to be other than a human being? After analyzing this question, "boom", reality kicked in, cigarettes are my pimp. They control everything I do. When I first wake up no matter what time it is the first thing I do is smoke a cigarette. Psychologically this is my wake up cigarette; it gives me the energy to brush my teeth and take a shower. After that shower the next cigarette is calling me because I feel good and clean so I light up in route to iron. After I am dressed another cigarette is calling me and that little voice assures me that every time I have a cigarette in my mouth I am protected: Yes, I actually believe that having that cigarette in my mouth is my security blanket. Then finally I make it to work or college. I am there twenty minutes at the most and the voice starts calling me again but I can't just leave my assigned work. As seconds pass my craving for cigarettes gets stronger and psychologically I can see a picture of me puffing on a good cigarette but physically there is no cigarette only the strong craving for one. Oh boy! Finally it's time for my break. The first cigarette I smoked burned so fast that I didn't enjoy it because emotionally I was drained and stressed out from the long forced waiting period. All this means is that I disobeyed that voice calling me, my pimp. So as an end result, I'll smoke enough cigarettes to make up for those missed, satisfying my pimp. I find that whenever I am upset, I'll smoke a cigarette because I believe that it relaxes me. And immediately after my meal or during a conversation, smoking a cigarette is mandatory. (Anonymous)

A second smoker relates:

At first it was social when I had a drink. I was surrounded by smokers which became a trigger to increase my habit. I thought that smoking with others would allow me to fit in. Anytime I got stressed personally or professionally, I had a cigarette. When I had the urge to smoke and I couldn't smoke immediately, I would become extremely agitated. There were periods when I experienced depression and low self esteem which led me to pick up a cigarette. If cigarettes were not available, there were times that I went to the grocery store any hour just to get my fix. After years of smoking, I experienced some health problems, but I kept smoking; I was addicted to cigarettes. I was unable to cope with any difficulties in life. Smoking was the only way I knew how to deal with uncomfortable feelings. Rather than face my issues, I would escape in smoking. (Anonymous)

A coffee addict relates:

I never took the time to put it in perspective but I, like many other people, have an addiction that I cannot control: Coffee. I start my day with a cup of coffee but not any coffee; it has to be strong. It is a ritual, a habit, a time to relax, a wake-up call, a way to keep me alert, a morning boost, a stress reliever because I don't know how my day is going to be. As I look back, I ask myself: How did this addiction start? Tracing back my moments, I remember being introduced to coffee by my grandmother. In my country it is normal for young children to have coffee with bread and butter. There have been times in my life that I have tried to stop but I end up going back to the same habit. People remind me that my mood changes when I don't have my coffee. I respond in a sarcastic way: Well we all have to die of something. There have been times when I would eat the coffee beans just to get a fix, but like an addict says, "I am not hooked on this, I only drink occasionally." Looking back, I realize that coffee had taken control of my life. (Anonymous)

A sugar addict relates:

My addiction is sugar: eating flavored candy, cream filled cakes and especially chocolates and peanut butter filled candies, vanilla filled cookies and caramels. It's my addiction because I can't do without it. I always have the thought in my mind of eating something sweet. I can't stop thinking about it. I think about it all of the time. And when I eat it I can't just have one or two; it has to be lots and lots of it, and don't forget the soda to go with it. When I eat candy I get a feeling and a sense of regeneration, pleasure, relief and joy because I have it, but I still want more. Although I know it is bad for me I can't avoid it. Candy and sweets are all over, in stores, supermarkets, street corners every where even at work. Knowing I have a problem I am unable to hide it. I am constantly fighting my desire to pick up. I may be in a store buying something else other than sweets, but there it is presenting itself, calling out to me: "Buy it, taste it, enjoy it." Sometimes I win the battle but most of the time I lose. Knowing what I did is wrong, the guilt settles in. I sometimes feel powerless over my actions, and for something as harmless as candy, but for me you see it is more than harmful. For me it could end up being the end because it could kill me slowly because I suffer from diabetes. (Anonymous)

A food addict relates:

I am a food addict. My addiction is a pathological disorder, a compulsive craving for food. I understand that eating certain foods may be harmful to my health but I eat anyway. This addiction causes me to crave food when I am not hungry. I consume larger amounts of food at one time. It causes me great stress, grief and mental pain. It is so easy to eat instead of figuring out the hurts in life: Why am I feeling this way, what can I do to stop the hurt, insecurities and frustrations? There are so many emotions that I feel that my heart and head often hurt. I smother these emotions by eating rather than analyzing them. My mind won't slow down; I can't sleep; I just want to live in a state of peace. I eat when I am feeling depressed, frustrated and lonely. It's a never ending cycle. What do I do? I need to eat to live, but I need to create a balance in my life. I realize that I am out of control. I understand that the way I choose to eat is harmful, but I continue this type of destructive behavior. When I give into my addiction, I am riddled with shame, guilt and failure. My foods of choice are fried foods, sweets, chips and chocolate. Sometimes I eat so fast, I don't stop to taste the food that I am eating. I have the same eating patterns over and over again. After eating something, I often feel disgusted with myself for falling off of the wagon again. (Anonymous)

A second food addict relates:

Everything I do revolves around food. It has been like this for as long as I can remember. Food has comforted me throughout my childhood, teenage years and into my adulthood. I Eat when I am not hungry, when I am happy, when I am depressed, and when I am anxious. I use food to cover up my loneliness and depression. In my mind food is my friend, my companion. My addiction to food has me gaining weight to the point that when I go shopping, nothing fits, which depresses me, so I eat and the cycle continues. I am in a marriage where there is no communication. My husband works nights and he makes me feel guilty if I want to go out with my friends, so I stay at home and eat. My uncontrollable weight has me taking medication for high blood pressure, hypothyroid and borderline diabetes, but I keep eating. I am a member of a gym where I can utilize equipment to aid in weight loss and I also joined Weight Watchers. I start a new diet everyday but I end up walking into Dunkin Donuts. I feel that I need to control my actions, but I can't. I use food to cover up my fears. I think it is better than using drugs, but in my mind, I know it is equally as dangerous. (Anonymous)

An adrenaline addict relates:

I started working out in college with my fraternity brothers and I never stopped. Working out has been such an integral part of my life. I get an adrenaline rush when I work out. I am not sure of what could replace it if it was ever taken away from me. I am an adrenaline junkie, whether it is from skydiving, snowboarding, waterskiing or riding my wave runner. The more dangerous the more rush. The rush is exhilarating and it makes me feel happy and alive when I am doing it. It is the only way I can relax and face the obstacles in my life. If I don't work out or do some physical activity, I feel anxious, irritable and sluggish. (Anonymous)

A relationship addict relates:

My addiction is being in relationships. I repeatedly become involved in one relationship after another. I gain a sense of thrill and excitement being in a relationship and falling in love over and over again. I continuously engage in destructive relationships. I become physically and mentally dependent on my partner and it does not allow me to function normally. I become obsessed when I sense the feeling of liking someone. I then pursue the person and I am already feeling myself falling in love before I even know the person. I try to impose myself into that person's daily activities and gain attachment. My obsession does not stop when my love for the person stops or the person stops loving me. I remain in the relationship because I am so emotionally attached. I cannot remember how many times I told someone I loved them and wanted to be with them and I knew it was a lie. When I am in a relationship, I immediately attach myself to that person and make my world into that person. I am fearful that my partner will leave me. To even think of ending the relationship results in paranoia, insomnia, anxiety, depression, nervousness, irritability and agitation. These feelings arise even if I don't like the person. With few exceptions, I gain excitement and a high from falling in love and I have stayed in emotionally abusive relationships to avoid losing that feeling. I feel worthless and depressed when I am not around my partner. I have emotionally abused some of my partners and I did not leave because I avoid losing relationships. I can not stop wanting the person I am with. If the person leaves me I do anything within my power to get them back; I feel like I can not live without them. When my friends and family confront me about my unhealthy relationships, I become angry and hostile. I have lost connections to friends, family and my self-worth due to my addiction. I have lost jobs, dropped out of school and battled with deep depression due to my addiction. I feel worthless if I am not in a relationship. Relationships define who I am. (Anonymous)

An addict to self defeating behavior relates:

I wish I could say I was addicted to a drug because that would seem more normal, however, what I am addicted to seems crazy and irrational even to me. I am addicted to self depreciating thoughts and behaviors. My obsession with my overall performance as a human being and the constant compulsion to tell myself I am not good enough in any capacity whether it be work, school or appearance is having an effect on my physical and mental health. Believing in my head and my heart that I am not good enough are affecting my marriage, my social life and is having a negative effect on my daily life as well. I have always had self esteem issues but over the past few years the negative feelings I have for myself are keeping me from living. While some people go for a drink, I go for telling myself that I can not do anything because I will fail, and I tell myself that over and over again throughout the course of every day. I don't know how this addiction started, but I know it is taking over my life. (Anonymous)

A control addict relates:

I would say that my addiction has to do with power and control. I need to feel that I am in control of all that happens around me. My addiction promotes self indulgence and often numbs me to the criticism of others. It promotes friendship with one class while despising others. It allows me to be aggressive in achieving my goals, while ignoring the feelings and concerns of others. When I am in control, I am on a high. In situations where I feel I have little or no control, my mood and attitude changes, and I am anxious and insecure. I know it is keeping me from being truly happy. I am turning into someone who would rather stay locked up inside of her apartment where I don't have to worry about failure. It's hard for me to struggle with something so intangible. No one knows how torturous this is for me. (Anonymous)

A food addict highlighted on Dr. Phil featuring Dr. Travis Stork relates:

I eat chalk; the chalk that you write on the chalkboard with. This is my first best friend - the chalk. If I am angry, sad, I would eat the whole thing. On an average day, I eat seven to nine sticks. For leisure, if I am on a train or a bus, I break this up, and then I'll just chew it and feel better. It's like candy. I love it. It's not unpleasant. It's very pleasant. It's my best friend. I have been eating chalk since I was 14... It makes me feel good. It helps me. It doesn't talk back to me. I run to the chalk. I hold it in my hand, and I just eat it, and it's my food. Usually, it will be my primary food. (E! Network's What's Eating You, Erasing Her Habit, October 13, 2010.)

The Internet, "You've Got Mail," is the ultimate in limiting physical contact and promoting the isolation that is reflective of addiction. Please note that there is a significant difference between "computer geeks" and those who have a dysfunctional relationship with the Internet. Internet abuse is abnormally excessive and can culminate in poor academic performance, job loss and divorce. Consider a two year study done by Carnegie Mellon University titled "Home Net." Research indicates that the more time one spends on the Internet, the less communication between family members, and friends. Reportedly, these relationships were compromised ultimately resulting in loneliness, isolation and depression.

It is the preoccupation, the obsessive-compulsive thoughts and cravings, the powerlessness, and the repetitive maladaptive behavior despite the consequences that constitute these behaviors as addictions. One must understand that the drug, the substance, the behavior, is symptomatic, the physical manifestation of an underlying problem. In other words, the substance which we use is the externalization of an internal state of dis-ease. Life is filled with challenges. "Living life on life terms" can be a balancing act. Often times we are overwhelmed with pain, resentment, emptiness, guilt or the highs and lows, ups and down of everyday living. Those problems are compounded by the attitude of society which perpetuates the notion that there is always something outside of our self that can make us feel better. And then of course we live in an overindulgent society where excess is the norm: more, more, more, higher, higher, higher. Delayed gratification is replaced with immediate satisfaction, symbolic of Freud's "Id": "I want it and I want it now." That quest has enabled many to sacrifice themselves, their families, friends and all that is good in their lives. Compounding the problem, is the mis-education and propaganda we have been fed. From the time we are born, through adolescence and adulthood; to the time we die, we are misinformed with the notion that the solution to any and all problems can be resolved with an external solution. We forget to teach our children that the power is within ourselves. Like Dorothy, in The Wizard of Oz, who traveled all over the Land of Oz looking for a way to get home. And all she had to do was be still, look into her heart, connect with her spirit and transcend her space in time, naturally, to get home. So we go through life searching. We learn maladaptive coping skills from our parents, our peers, and the media.

Children in particular don't just become addicts overnight. In these times, they are faced with tough challenges and decisions at increasingly younger and more vulnerable ages. The following is in relation to drugs:

> My introduction to drugs was something that I didn't see coming. I was pretty confused about a lot of things, no matter what I did, it always seemed as if I was bored; I saw a gateway, something different. "Why didn't anyone tell me about the iron bars?" Well they didn't tell me until it was too late. From that night, there would never be another gate for me. No one told me that by the very first time, it is too late. You see in my case, I was a junkie from the very beginning. By eleven, there wasn't a drug I hadn't tried. By age twelve, there wasn't a drug I hadn't sold. By age thirteen, I found a new gateway: iron bars: busted: four B Felonies for Sales and Possession. (Anonymous Recovering Addict)

Mediums of Indoctrination: A Culture Embedded With Drug References and Realities

Even the word "addicted," for some, can conjure up a particular state of mind. Consider a Macy's ad in the New York Times, (10/02), promoting a new cologne called "Dior Addicted," depicted by a sensuous, scantily clad model. One must not only look at the visual but consider the message, "Live your most daring dreams." Perhaps an over simplification for some, but again it is the attitude, the notion that addiction is a normal aspiration of life. In reality, our addictions deter us away from our dreams.

Addicted attitudes and messages permeate our society and we are not even aware of the insidious messages that are subliminally planted into our subconscious sometimes through the most unlikely mediums. It is suggested, and agreed by many, deemed unlikely by others, that there are a number of drug references in our children's classical fairy tales. "Snow White and the Seven Dwarfs," "Jack and the Bean Stalk," "Alice in Wonderland,"

"Rumpestiltskin," are just some of the fairy tales with drug innuendoes. The actual reference to drugs in Disney's "Snow White and the Seven Dwarfs," has been associated with cocaine. Snow White represents cocaine and the Seven Dwarfs: Happy, Sneezy, Sleepy, Grumpy, Bashful, Dopey and Doc represent the stages one goes through while under the influence of cocaine. It is interesting to note that "Snow White," or "Snow," is an alias for cocaine. In an article by CannabisCulture.Com titled "Stoned Fairy Tales," ascension up the beanstalk in "Jack and the Beanstalk," is symbolic of Jack getting "high."Reportedly, the beans Jack receives represents the marijuana seeds which can quickly grow into a tall plant. The term "bean," was commonly used as a euphemism for cannabis seeds during Europe's Middle Ages. Interestingly, the reference to drugs in "Jack and the Beanstalk" continues as his addiction becomes more progressive, he engages in more risk taking behavior, as he steals more and more, until ultimately he tries to steal the "golden harp," which almost leads to his demise (overdose). Jack finally cuts the beanstalk down, which is paralleled to him overcoming his drug addiction.

In "RumpelStiltskin," the power of drugs is implied when the maiden becomes a queen after the dwarf spins hemp straw into gold. The extreme consequences of addiction are seen as she first gives up her necklace, then ring, followed by her agreement to sacrifice her first born child.

In the "Wizard of Oz," reference is made to "midgets" and "poppies." One may remember that Dorothy fell into a deep sleep while running through the poppy fields, consistent with the effects of the opium poppy plant.

In Walt Disney's movie, "Alice in Wonderland," reference is made to Alice falling "down the rabbit hole" which is apparently a metaphor to taking drugs. Reference is also made to Alice drinking a potion which has the ability to make one very big or very small, commonly known illusions manifested with psychedelic drugs.

Drug references are also made in relation to many fairy tales and cartoons as it relates to the "Amanita Muscaria" which is a psychedelic mushroom that can cause delirium. The mushroom provides shelter for the "Smurfs," a very popular cartoon which gained popularity in the 1980's. One may also reference the mega hit video game called "Super Mario Brothers" which not only utilizes the mushroom but has named it; they call the mushroom, "Toad." One may reference, Snopes.com, Cannabisculture.Com for further references to the parallel between children's fairy tales and drugs.

Admittedly, some references extend the imagination beyond belief and to some any parallel between fairytales and anything drug related is a bizarre absurdity. Certainly the innocence of a child's mind sees and hears these fairytales as pure entertainment and fantasy. In fact, on a cognitive level, a child does not even have the capacity to think logically or interpret metaphors which are abstractions of reality. Unfortunately, however, older children and adults have been somewhat corrupted by a society enmeshed with drugs.

One must also consider that the stark reality is that many of our fairy tales and adventures were created by authors who were in fact, under the influence of drugs when they created these timeless master pieces. Reportedly, Lewis Carroll, the author whose book "Alice in Wonderland" was adapted, was an opium user. The famous writer Edger Allen Poe was also known to use drugs. According to the Sunday times, March 20, 2005, and a BBC program, "The Adventures of Robert Louis Stevenson," the famed author of "Dr. Jekyll and Mr. Hyde," was under the influence of a hallucinogenic drug which was used repeatedly on him as a treatment for bleeding during the Victorian Era. One may remember that in the adventure, the good Dr. Jekyll takes a drug that transforms him into Mr. Hyde who represents the evil side of the psyche. It is quite likely that the alteration of his personality brought on by the psychedelic drug was a significant influence on his writings.

Certainly the influence of mind altering substances on the creators of children's fairy tales does not substantiate the metaphoric parallels between them and the drug, however, by the very nature of the dialogue as to the realities of such assertions as well as the fact that often times one's creativities can be effected by drug usage, it calls upon one to at least look at the pervasiveness of drugs within our society and the potential to effect us on so many levels.

American music leaves much less to speculation as it relates to its association with a drug culture. Irrespective of which genre of music one references, the common theme in many songs revolves around drugs. The Blues, Rock In Roll, R&B and Rap are laden with references to drugs. The range falls into a perfect dichotomy with songs either glamorizing or promoting drugs to those songs which address the sickness and pain that accompanies addiction. Our music is important because it reflects our psyche, our state of mind, as well as our experiences and social realities. Let's for a moment, journey into the lyrics of some of the songs which reflect our attitudes and effect our behavior.

Jefferson Airplane's song "White Rabbit," actually bridges the gap between fairy tale and music as he references, "Alice in Wonderland." His lyrics speak to the hallucinogenic effects of psychedelic drugs. He brings light to pills that make one as tall as ten feet and then others that can make one small. Inanimate objects from a chest board come alive and the ingestion of mushrooms alter one's mind.

One may remember the Temptations: They had many songs that spoke to the allure of drugs. "Psychedelic Shack" guaranteed a place which could blow one's mind, a place where everyone and anyone could go for relief. One could either commune with others or do some self introspection. It's a place where one could be any thing imagined. "Ball of Confusion," spoke to the political and social "confusion" as well as the prevalence of drugs in the 1970's. The lyrics referenced the popularity and sales of pills and the euphoria which distracted one from reality. The lyrics of "Cloud Nine" also allowed one to escape the harsh realities of life. Just as in "Psychedelic Shack," it offered an escape, where one could be what one wanted to be, that is free from any responsibilities, millions of miles from any earthly realities.

The artist Marvin Gaye's song, "Flyin High in the Friendly Sky," dealt with heroin addiction as illustrated in his lyrics when he referenced being hooked to the boy who could potentially emasculate men. Marvin Gaye like the Temptations sang about the 70's, a time laden with heroin addiction which had a profound effect among our inner city communities as well as our Vietnam Veterans. The reference to "boy" in his lyrics is an alias for heroin. His lyrics further spoke to heroin's promise of euphoria, the insanity of abusing, and the addictive nature of heroin.

Rick James released a song in 1978 entitled "Mary Jane." Mary Jane is an alias for marijuana. In his song, Rick James affirmed his love for "Mary Jane." He spoke of his admiration for "Mary Jane" which could elevate him from his lows and take him to paradise.

Musical Youth, a British group popularized a song in the 80's called "Pass the Dutchie," which was a cover version of a song by the Mighty Diamonds called, "Pass the Koutchie." "Duthchie" or "Dutch" is a reference to a "blunt" which is marijuana rolled up in a Dutch Masters Cigar.

One can see how marijuana was totally infused in the life of the artist Afroman, who sang the song, "Because I Got High." The song also illuminates the consequences of abusing marijuana including the a-motivational qualities of the drug, the effects it has on grades and employment, poor decision making, and the severe consequences that can ensue. Afroman's lyrics relate all of the things he was going to do. He referenced his intention to cleaning his room, going to class, going to work, going to court, paying his car note, etc., etc., etc. The lyrics take on an even sadder note when they reference the consequences of becoming a paraplegic and messing up one's life all for the sake of getting high.

The group, Cypress Hill, also referenced marijuana in their song, "Hits From the Bong." They sang about how you use it and their love for it. A perfect dichotomy was also presented between fun and games and the insanity of the disease; bleeding, desperate, and reduced to an animal living in a jungle.

The artists, Metallica, also spoke to the obsession and pain of addiction in their song, "Master of Puppets." Their lyrics addressed the destruction of one's life that crumbles and bows to a master called drugs.

Eric Clapton's song, "Cocaine," feminized the drug and offered it as an ultimate companion, an ultimate solution to any and all blues.

Cocaine was also referenced by the group, Sugar Hill Gang, who sang the song, "White Lines," which spoke to the journey and inevitable destruction of using the drug. In the beginning one is enamored by the drug's effect only to end up brain dead (not literally) but spiritually bankrupt.

For our younger readers, Lil' Wayne's song, "I Feel Like Dying," speaks to the positive experience he has with drugs. For Lil' Wayne, drinking and drugging are the ultimate state of consciousness. His lyrics glamorize wine, marijuana, codeine and Xanax. The euphoria he achieves from using transcends him above all others, on the same plain as the stars, the moon and Mars. The security and serenity of codeine; the total surrender to Xanax is the ultimate high and his only destruction is the temporary lack of availability.

Jay Z's song, "I Know," makes reference to Sugar Hill, Black Rain, China White, all drug innuendoes. His lyrics address heroin addiction including the obsession, the struggle for abstinence and the pain of withdrawal.

The artist, 50 Cents,' song, "A Baltimore Love Thing," also addresses heroin addiction. The lyrics speaks to the obsession, how one uses it, the euphoria, withdrawal, and ultimate destruction that comes along with it.

Snoop Dogg, "The legal card carrying icon of marijuana," is known for glamorizing and promoting the drug. His songs include, but are not limited to: "Smoke Weed Everyday," "Smokin' Smoken Weed," "Money 2 Fold," "DP Gagsta," "Chin Check," "Ain't Nut'in Personal," "Get It Up," "It's a Beautiful Thing," "The One and Only," "20 Dollars to My Name," "Press Play," "Next Episode": The list is endless!

The artist Ja Rule promoted ecstasy and marijuana in his lyrics which spoke to his sexual prowess, the transcendental state, as well as his thirst for Evian water, a necessity because of the dehydration caused from Ecstasy.

In addition, one may remember the summer young kids and young adults were snapping their fingers to Snoop's lyrics: "Rollin' down the street, smokin' indo, and sippin on gin and juice." One can also not forget the glamorization of the cognac Alize, included in the lyrics of Queen Latifah, Keith Sweat, and Dr. Dre.

There are many other artists whose songs delved into the world of drugs and addiction, from Cab Calloway's "Reefer Man" to Nikki Sixx of Motley Crue who produced an album, "The Heroin Diaries: A Year in the Life of a Shattered Rock Star"; The Velvet Underground song, "Heroin" which talks about the use and effects of heroin; Neil Young, "The Needle and the Damage Done," references the musicians he knew who abused heroin; David Bowie's, "Space Oddity" and "Ashes to Ashes" that specifically referenced a "Junkie" strung out on "heaven's high/hitting an all time low"; Rozz William's, "The Whorse's Mouth,"dealt with his heroin addiction; and Anthony Kiedis of the Red Hot Chili Peppers wrote about his addiction in his auto-biography, "Scar Tissue," just to name a few.

In addition to our music, American culture has been infused with drugs and drug culture through our movies. In 1916, "The Mystery of the Leaping Fish" dealt with cocaine and opium; in 1955, Otto Preminger's, "The Man with the Golden Arm," played by Frank Sinatra, dealt with heroin addiction; in 1994, Quentin Tarantino's, "Pulp Fiction," starring John Travolta and Uma Thurman who OD's from snorting drugs, demonstrates the "how to's" of shooting heroin; in 2000, Darren Aronosfky, "Requiem for a Dream," depicts heroin addiction; "Candy," with Heath Ledger, illustrates the destruction of heroin abuse; James St. James' movie, "Party Monster" is a true story depicting out of control club kids who abuse heroin, Special K, and cocaine; and "Gia," a movie based on the real life model Gia Carangi chronicles her addiction. In 1971, "Panic In Needle Park," with Al Pachino, depicts real life scenes of users injecting heroin; the movie, "Things We Lost in the Fire," with Benicio Del Toro looks at his struggle to overcome his addiction; the movie "Blow," with Johnny Depp and Penelope Cruz highlighted the story of George Jung, a major contributor to the cocaine drug trade in the 70's, and I am sure one remembers the film "American Gangster," based on the story of Frank Lucas' heroin drug trade. In addition, one can look at a number of TV series which glamorize drinking and/or deal with addiction. Shows like A & E's, "Intervention," VH1's, "Celebrity Rehab," and TLC's, "My Strange Addiction" address the sickness of addiction.

Our America: Our culture: Our lives. It's ironic that drug addiction is considered deviant behavior and we have little tolerance for drug abusers. If one considers that everything is relative, drugs are more a cultural norm than a violation there of. One tends to look at isolated incidents and behavior which only succeeds in minimizing the gravity of the problem. Drug innuendoes, the glamorization and promotion of drugs, the reality of drug addiction is a social reality that can no longer be denied. It is so enmeshed in our advertisements, our fairytales, our cartoons, our music, our videos and our movies that we have truly become desensitized to the harsh realities of its destruction. One more person afflicted with drugs, one more person bites the dust. But it is not just one more. Collectively we are losing the battle. Like a Trojan horse it stands before us, consuming us, spewing invisible rays of destruction and death. We are at war America, and like that Trojan horse, it appears to be a war against drugs. In reality it's a war not against, but for our spirits. We are losing our ground because we have become disconnected from our inner strength. We are so comfortable with the immediate gratification of the here and now, we have become so allured by the immediate anesthetization of the pain of our past and of our present, that we have resigned ourselves to self defeating behavior. The only way we will win the war is to reclaim our spirit and hold steady to our natural inclination of self preservation. We must get honest; we must take a stance. Enough is enough, stop the madness. I will no longer allow the ill promises of drugs and other behaviors that allow me to transcend this place and time to consume me. I reclaim my spirit; right here, right now.

CHAPTER 3: ALCOHOL IS A DRUG!

Trends

America, our daughters are soaking tampons in Vodka and inserting them into their vaginal cavity and our sons are inserting those same Vodka tampons into their rectum! Too graphic for you? Good. It is imperative that one is aware of the severity of the problem. This trend that has substantially increased during the last few years is appealing because it alleviates the smell of alcohol on the breath. One may reference a song by VIC Chesutt in 2003, called "Band Camp," which glamorizes the intoxicating effects of Vodka soaked tampons: "Once you soak a tampon in some Vodka, wore it to school second period science lab you fell off your stool."

Inserting Vodka soaked tampons into the vaginal and rectal cavity is also appealing because alcohol absorbed through the mucous membranes is a fast route of administration which allows the chemical to enter the blood stream and travel to the brain and throughout every system in the body. Besides intoxification, there are obvious dangers in introducing a foreign substance into the vaginal cavity. Particularly in young women, the natural ph balance which protects against infections is compromised and the chemicals in the alcohol can cause burning, bleeding and ultimately can damage one's reproductive organs. Another little crafty method used by our boys is inserting a tube attached to a funnel into their rectum and pouring beer down the funnel. Alcohol absorbed across the mucous membranes has also been reported by a substance abuse treatment center in Arizona, where reportedly children as young as twelve years old are snorting vodka through their nose. Our children engage in these practices because they are resourceful and they believe it is fun.

And just when you thought you had heard enough, another interesting fad that our children are engaging in is called Vodka eyeballing or Vodka eye shots. Yes, it is just what you think. Kids are pouring Vodka into their eyes to get high. Specifically, you close one eye with a finger and pour the Vodka into the other eye. According to the UK Daily Mail, the trend began in the USA and is becoming increasingly popular in England. According to a Fox News Report (May 25, 2010), "The fad sometimes starts out as a dare before or after intoxification." A Washington, D.C. Newspaper states,

> when vodka touches the eye, it destroys the sensitive top layer … initially causes pain and then causing tiny scratches that will gradually go away over a period of 1-3 days. Vision can appear blurry during healing, and scratches can become permanent if the process is repeated. Vodka will then seep into sinuses via tear ducts and dissolve into the bloodstream, damaging the mucous membrane along the way.

A Maryland optometrist compared eyeballing to an alcohol enema. "In essence, you could melt the cornea."

Another interesting and dangerous trend our youths are engaging in is drinking alcohol from hand sanitizers. Generally, hand sanitizers are approximately 62% alcohol in contrast to wine for example, which contains 12% alcohol. Two ounces of hand sanitizers is equivalent to four shots of Vodka and at a fraction of the cost. Reports from the American Association of Poison Control indicate that in 2006, over 12,000 children were poisoned by hand sanitizers. "The fruity smells are particularly appealing to younger children who use the hand sanitizers and then lick their hands which can potentially lead to alcohol poisoning". One must keep in mind that the younger you are the less ability you have to metabolize this toxin, so the implications of toddlers and young children ingesting sanitizers has a potentially profound effect. The trend among older children and adolescents is also a source of great alarm.

One's resourcefulness for absorbing alcohol does not stop with Vodka soaked tampon, rectum beer funnels, Vodka eyeballing or hand sanitizers. We have also developed an ingenious way of inhaling alcohol. Inhalation happens to be the fastest route of administration taking all of 7-10 seconds to take effect. The chemical enters the lungs, is absorbed into the blood stream, and travels directly to the nervous system including the brain. There are a few methods of inhaling alcohol that I am aware of as of to date. With the ingenuity of our young, the possibility of another method will have become popularized by the time one reads this text. One method is to take dry ice which contains carbon dioxide, pour alcohol over it and inhale the vapors through your nose and mouth. The second method is using a "Hookah" like device. The "Hookah" is a water pipe device which originated in India and is a staple in Turkish and Middle Eastern Cultures. If one travels through certain ethnic areas around the city, one may have noticed large, beautifully adorned pipes in the windows of many establishments. There are also many "Hookah" bars in Manhattan, that attract our young who partake of the "Hookah" as a socially acceptable ritual. This modern day version of using the "Hookah" has become popular for inhaling alcohol. A third method is using a newly designed device that vaporizes alcohol so that one can inhale the fumes with the express purpose of getting high. The device looks very similar to an asthma pump and promises intoxification without the burn or smell. These methods have become alluring because of their immediate effects with the fringe benefit of no calories, no hangover and it is cheaper than buying alcohol.

Unfortunately, in the quest for a good time and to alter one's state of consciousness, our young are not in tuned to the harmful effects these methods of inhalation have on the body and the mind. Specifically, the heart rate is increased, there is vomiting, slurred speech, loss of coordination, hallucinations, delusions, memory loss and imminent brain damage. Another ingenious method of absorbing alcohol is achieved with the use of Vodka bongs/bombs. This method is a form of binge drinking. Alcohol is consumed orally at a fast rate. Because alcohol requires no digestion, it is absorbed almost immediately through the small intestine. The bong delivers 10X more alcohol than a person would drink in one serving. The consequences can be fatal, but of course one has nothing to worry about because "alcohol is not a drug."

Binge Drinking

When one looks at the trends in relation to alcohol consumption, the glaring reality of binge drinking among our college students is alarming. Consider fraternity initiation practice among young boys who consume as many consecutive shots of liquor as possible with the ultimate goal of being the last man standing in order to demonstrate their prowess as an acceptable and worthy candidate into the fraternity. When one considers that you only metabolize 1/2 ounce per hour, the excessive amounts of alcohol consumed in such a short period of time can be fatal. According to Bloch (2006), "Binge drinking remains in excess of 40% among college students and more than 1,700 college students died in alcohol related incidents." In addition, according to Lynch (2007), "In 2003, motor vehicle accidents were the leading cause of death in college youth in the United States. More than a third of the US college student drivers reported drinking and driving in the past month." Furthermore, statistics indicate that college students are far more likely to drink excessively than those individuals of the similar age who are not in college. What is even more alarming is that our colleges seem to condone such maladaptive behavior by making alcohol accessible to students. Drive through many college towns throughout America and examine the liquor sales promotions within that college community. Drinking establishments open early and close late; there are special promotions with drinking specials at nominal rates, and the drinks are often served in oversized glasses, pitchers and even fish bowls. In addition, one should reference a web site called, "Boys Icing Boys" to see the excessive and dangerous drinking patterns that are consumed and encouraged by college students. Reportedly, "College boys carry around cans of Smirnoff Ice and challenge other boys who become marks. Following the challenge, the mark must get down on one knee and chug down the Ice. If your mark has his own can of Ice in his possession, the original boy must drink both his own can and the can of the mark. The boys are carrying the Smirnoff Ice in fanny packs, in the glove compartment of their vehicles and are even sending them through Fed Ex to places of business. Despite the inappropriateness of the challenge, one can not refuse as it demonstrates an ultimate "Ice insult" culminating in excommunication from the group." Binge drinking among college students is further exacerbated by clever advertisers who maniacally and ubiquitously plant subliminal messages promoting drinking. According to Valerie D'Alessandro, "They advertise through sponsoring sports, rock concerts and parties, as well as promotional activities that take place at local bars." Reportedly, "It is not hard to target college students because all the industry has to do is offer free or cheap beer, and students will participate. They sponsor contests during promotional activities and they make it an all around good time for the students." The impact of advertising on binge drinking is also highlighted in an article by Michele Mariani, who references a 1999 Federal Trade Commission report which pointed to alcohol advertising as one reason why as many as a third of high school seniors and 40% of college students are binge drinkers. In addition, according to a (2012) article in the New York Times, one in every six Americans binges at least four times a month.

Traffic Fatalities

Unfortunately, traffic fatalities go beyond the college communities. In 2008, the National Highway Traffic Safety Administration published the following drunk driving car accidents:

There were 11,773 drunken driving deaths in 2008 which accounted for a 32% of the total amount of car accident deaths. 1,347 children ages 14 and younger died as occupants in car accidents. Of those deaths 216 (approximately 16%) were the direct result of drunk drivers. Along with the 1,347 child occupant fatalities another 34 children died as pedestrians or bikers who were hit by drunk drivers. Night time drivers were four times more likely to die in drunk driving crashes than those driving during the daytime. Weekend drivers were twice as likely to be involved in drinking and driving crashes than weekday drivers. Twenty-one to twenty-four age group accounted for 34% of all alcohol impaired drivers who died in accidents. The twenty-five to thirty-four demographic accounted for 31% while those from thirty-five to forty-four years of age accounted for 25%. (NHTSA, 2008)

We as citizens must assume responsibility and refrain from drinking and driving. One may remember the Taconic Parkway crash in New York on July 20, 09, where a mother drove the wrong way on the parkway killing eight people. According to autopsy reports, a large percentage of alcohol and THC were discovered in her blood.

In October of 09, an 11 year old Manhattan, New York girl, Leandra Rosado was killed when the driver of her car crashed on the Henry Hudson Parkway. Consequently, the Leandra's Law enacted on December 2009 mandates that driving drunk with a child in the car is an automatic felony. According to the New York Daily News (12/17/09), "The law makes it a felony, punishable by up to four years in prison to drive with a blood alcohol content of at least .08, with a youngster 15 or under in the car. Drunk drivers who cause the death of a child riding in their car will face up to 25 years in prison. Those who seriously injure a child passenger in a DWI crash will face up to 15 years." On August 15, 2010, the second part of Leandra's Law went into effect which mandates felons to install a "breathalyzer box," in their car which requires them to pass a breathalyzer before they can drive. If the BAC is .025 or over the ignition will lock. The cost of $200 paid by the felon includes installation, GPS, camera, and maintenance fee. Apparently,

Rudy Cota, the first drunk driver to be convicted under the law, did not get it. Sadly, neither are Yvonne Merrino Doyon-Brush, driving with a nine year old, John P. Catone, driving with a one in a half year old, Jack R. Cole Jr. driving with a three month old infant, or a seventeen year old driving with his fifteen year old girl friend. All parties have been convicted under the Leandra's Law.

In Prince George's County, Maryland, February 19, 2010, two parties involved in a fender bender stopped to exchange information, and in the process were fatally struck by a third vehicle: a driver under the influence. Not long after this fatal accident, on March 9, 2010, another child was killed in an alcohol related driving accident in Houston, Texas. According to The National Highway Traffic Safety Administration, "300 people are killed in wrong way driving crashes every year by drunk drivers."

Police Accountability

Blatant irresponsibility is also demonstrated by our nations finest. Police officers who pledge to protect and serve hide behind the "blue wall of silence", and blatantly lie to protect fellow officers. One may remember Andrew Kelly, a New York police officer, who was charged with drunk driving and vehicular manslaughter. Reports from the New York Post (10/1/09) indicate that officer Kelly mowed down and killed a pedestrian while under the influence of alcohol. Despite the fact that he reeked of booze, had slurred speech and glassy eyes, he was allowed to manipulate the system to his advantage by refusing to take a breathalyzer test. It was not until seven hours later, under court order, that Officer Kelly was mandated to take a blood alcohol test. Within that period the alcohol had a chance to metabolize; consequently, the blood test showed no evidence of alcohol in the officer's system. The manipulation of the facts pertaining to this case is a gross miscarriage of justice. The Kelly case is one in a series of incidents where police officers both on and off duty have engaged in dangerous and fatal behavior while under the influence of alcohol. Police officers must be held accountable to the same extent as any other American citizen. How many innocent people have to die before we say "enough is enough?" It is noteworthy, that on September 8, 2010, Andrew Kelly after giving up his badge just a few days before, pleaded guilty in the case, and on September 27, 2010, he was sentenced to 90 days in jail and five years probation.

Health Care Cost and Consequences

The health care cost of alcoholism is still another harsh reality that one must consider. According to the Columbia University Center for Addiction and Substance Abuse:

25-40% of all patients in US hospital beds are being treated for complications of alcohol related problems. Annual health care expenses for alcohol related problems amount to $22.5 billion. The total cost of alcohol problems is 175.9 billion a year.

In addition the following facts are important to note:

Untreated alcohol problems waste an estimated 184.6 billion dollars per year in healthcare, business and criminal justice cost and cause 100,000 deaths. Health care cost related to alcohol abuse is not limited to the user. Children of alcoholics who are admitted to the hospital average 62% more hospital days and 29% longer stays.

Alcohol use by underage drinkers results in 3.7 billion a year in medical care cost due to traffic crashes, violent crime, suicide attempts and other related consequences. The total annual cost of alcohol use by underage youth is 52.8 billion. Alcohol related car crashes are the number one killer of teens.

Alcohol use is also associated with, the next three leading causes of death among the young: homicide, suicide, and drowning.

Alcohol is the drug most frequently used by 12 to 17 year olds and the one that causes the most negative health consequences. More than 4 million adolescents under the legal drinking age consume alcohol in any given month (<u>Columbia University, 1994</u>). Concurrently, a National Survey on Drug Use and Health conducted by Substance Abuse and Mental Health Services (SAMHSA) dated December 10, 2009, indicate that "86.1 percent had used alcohol in their lifetime, including 62.8 percent who had initiated use before their 18th birthday." A second report by the same source dated April 1, 2010, indicated that, "Drinkers 12-20 purchased their own alcohol."

CHAPTER 4: ALCOHOL IS A DRUG: FROM ANOTHER PERSPECTIVE

Societal Attitude and Perception: "Stupid Thinking: Stupid Drinking"

Every semester a very popular class called Alcohol Drugs and Behavior is taught at the college. Eager students flock to the class either because it is a really interesting subject, or they have family members who are effected by the disease of addiction, or because they're part of the club scene, getting high, or simply because they identify with the topic and believe: How hard could this class be? To their surprise they are very quickly confronted with the reality that the class is indeed challenging as they are hit with the first thought provoking question: What is wrong with the title of this class? Not to my surprise, they are dumb founded just as many other Americans. Even in the world of academia, on a college level, one continues to disassociate alcohol from drugs. In reality a more accurate title for the class is Drugs and Behavior.

America, alcohol is a drug. If one is still not convinced by the addictive behaviors of our children and adolescents, if the illogical, irrational and irresponsible behavior of those who are abusing alcohol is not a valid indicator, if fatalities and health care costs are not alarming, if the emotional and physical abuse and deterioration of family systems don't encourage one to look at alcohol abuse more seriously, the following are some basic facts for one to consider about this drug that is called alcohol.

Alcohol is one of the oldest and most widely used psychoactive drugs:

Yes, I said drug! As a species, we have been consuming alcohol for more than 5000 years. Our perception of alcohol as a drug is distorted by our historical and intimate relationship to the substance. It is legal, available, and an integral part of our culture. Exacerbating the problem is society's attitude in relation to alcohol. There are common misconceptions that promote alcohol drinking. The notion is that every one drinks; the more a man is able to drink, the more "machismo" he is; drinking makes women feel more sensuous and alluring. Ladies, have you ever seen an intoxicated man at a bar and said, "wow," he's hot! "He can really hold his liquor! He's a real man!" Gentleman, have you ever been at a club and seen an intoxicated woman? Many thoughts may have crossed your mind, but the idea that she was a classy woman whom you would like to meet was not one of them! Other common misconceptions about alcohol promote the idea that alcohol is some how associated with wealth and prominence. There is certainly some validity in the notion that the more money one has, the higher quality of alcohol one consumes. One is reminded of the previous reference to Puff Daddy who was known some time ago for his preference for Cristal, a very expensive champagne. One is also assured that people of affluence gravitate to certain alcoholic beverages but the attitude of the general population that in some way their association with these beverages indicates an air of superiority constitutes a gross misconception.

Alcohol the Drug

Alcohol is in fact an alluring drug. Its tranquilizing qualities potentially make one feel good and drinking is a vehicle which allows one to escape as the emotional and physical pain is anesthetized, but it is not without risk. Alcohol is a major depressant which slows down the central nervous system. The substance that makes alcohol a drug is ethyl alcohol, a thin colorless fluid. It is the least toxic within a family of alcohols including methyl alcohol which we use as an industrial solvent, isopropyl alcohol which is more than likely in one's medicine cabinet, and butyl alcohol which is an industrial solvent. The focus will be on ethyl alcohol. Note, however, that a desperate alcoholic will consume other forms of alcohol despite the imminent and obvious dangers.

Americans consume various types of alcoholic beverages. Beer, for example is derived from fermented grains such as corn, wheat, barley, and rye. Wine is produced from fermented fruit including grapes. Other alcoholic beverages (distilled spirits) such as whiskey, brandy, vodka, gin, are produced from fermented mixtures of cereal grains, vegetables, etc.

Physiological Aspects

Alcohol is unique because it requires no digestion. It is distributed through the walls of the gastrointestinal track including the mouth and the stomach. It is absorbed by blood vessels and capillaries into the small intestine which is the major absorption site. From there it is transported by the blood stream throughout the entire body. Alcohol is structurally non specific so it goes to every cell and every organ throughout the body. The alcohol is metabolized in the liver through an oxidation process where it is turned into carbon monoxide, water and energy. The alcohol will continue circulating through the liver and through out all parts of the body until all of the alcohol is oxidized. Remember, one can only metabolize ½ oz per hour. There are many factors that influence the metabolization of alcohol. Firstly, men are more efficient at metabolizing alcohol than their female counterpart because of the presence of an enzyme in their stomach called alcohol dehydrogenase which helps to break down the alcohol; consequently, alcohol is absorbed into the blood stream at a slower rate.

One must remember that alcohol is a toxic substance: It is a poison. The only reason one does not die is because of the biotransformation process that was just discussed. Through that process alcohol is detoxified and eliminated from our bodies by excretion including perspiration, urine, feces and vomit. During the process of distribution, alcohol reigns havoc on the brain. Consider the fact that the brain is the central command center of the body integrating and coordinating all bodily functions. The nervous system including the brain communicates through electro-chemical messages. Not only does alcohol block transmission but it temporarily depresses and paralyzes different parts of the brain. Consequently, bodily task coordinated by that part of the brain are also compromised. For example, the cerebral cortex is the higher functioning part of the brain which controls memory, reasoning and judgment. That is why under the influence of alcohol one does not always make the most adaptive decisions. One may also notice that intoxicated individuals can be confused and disoriented or they may stumble or fall because of poor coordination. The part of the brain that integrates these activities is the medulla. Once again, alcohol has depressed its functioning and as a result that behavior is compromised.

Short and Long Term Effects

Although the body has the capacity to detoxify alcohol, often the rate, frequency and patterns of drinking have a profound effect on the body. Even social or moderate consumption can have an adverse effect on individuals. For example, alcohol effects one's sensation and perception including tasks like visual and hearing acuity, alteration of senses, underestimation of speed of moving objects (cars), and alteration of one's sensitivity to odors and taste. In addition, the lower portion of the brain, specifically the limbic system is compromised which controls emotions such as happiness, fear and anger. Sleeping patterns are also interrupted: Initially sleep may be induced because of the depressant qualities but over the long run it interferes with REM, an acronym for rapid eye movement, which is our dream like restorative sleep cycle. Motor skills are also impaired; our kidneys produce more urine and of course the all too popular hangover are just some of the consequences of drinking.

Long term effects of drinking are more pervasive on a physiological, neurochemical and cellular level. They may include gastrointestinal system disorders, liver disease including the accumulation of fatty acids to cirrhosis of the liver, nervous system disease including but not limited to cognitive deficits, dementia, and Wernicke's Syndrome which is a thiamine (vitamin B) deficiency. This disorder leads to disorientation, delirium, impairment or paralysis of nerves related to motor movement including eye and muscular coordination. Thiamine deficiency can also lead to Korsakoff's psychosis, an alteration of one's personality. Long term effects can also include endocrine system disorders, mental disorders, cancer and death.

One must also consider the consequences of women who drink while they are pregnant. Many are aware that the child of an alcoholic can be born physically dependent on alcohol and even suffer from withdrawal symptoms. The infant may also be born with fetal alcohol syndrome or fetal alcohol effects. Consequently, they may suffer with nervous system disorders, structural and facial abnormalities, and growth deficiencies. Fetal alcohol syndrome is also the leading cause of mental retardation. Ironically, there was a point in time when doctors condoned moderate drinking to expectant mothers. Even today there are some physicians who support that notion. The reality is that no one can tell you how much is too much. There are alcoholic mothers who give birth to children born with out traces of fetal alcohol syndrome and then there are cases where mothers drank moderately and their child was born with this disorder. Certainly there are other complex factors which influence the prevalence of the syndrome; however, consider the facts. If alcohol is toxic for adults, it is certainly toxic for the fetus whose organs are not developed to the extent in which they have the capacity to metabolize alcohol. The consequences therefore, can be potentially severe.

CHAPTER 5: ALCOHOL IS A DRUG: FOR REAL

Personal Accounts of Alcoholics and Their Prisoners

If one is still not convinced of the seriousness of the disease of addiction, consider the following personal accounts of those who have personally suffered from the disease or those who have suffered at the hands of alcoholics:

I am a child of an alcoholic. I watched my father physically and emotionally abuse my mother until her spirit was broken. I watched my mother cater to him so that the blows would not come as often. I watched as my oldest brother made several attempts to come back home to live, only to be abused and pushed further away. I remember the blood stained pillows that my mother used to support my brothers back after my father tied him to a tree and whipped him across his back until he bled. I remember the blood that poured from my brother's nose after my father hit him across the face with a wrench and broke his nose. I remember how my father spoke of other people's children and compared them to his own, stating we were nothing and would never amount to anything. I remember leaving home at 17, hurt and bruised. (Anonymous adult child of an alcoholic)

A second account reads:

My family was complicated by alcoholism, long before the family knew what alcoholism was. What we did know about alcohol was that it made my father crazy. He never drank during the week, only on the weekends; then he would wreak havoc on all of us. We witnessed this man become Dr. Jekyll and Mr. Hyde. Once he came home drunk, pulled my mother out of the bed and commenced beating her. He broke her ribs and made her lie to the doctor saying that she had fallen down the stairs. He ran us from the house several times, chasing us with a loaded gun. As we got older we managed to intercept my father from hitting my mother. We four girls and two boys were able to pin him down and scream at him to stop and he did. But then he focused his attention on all of us, mostly me, because I showed less fear. I left home at the beginning of my senior year in high school with bruises up and down my right side because my father pulled a chair from under me, causing me to fall hard against the door behind me; in one motion he brought the chair down on my head. After the chair incident, I couldn't deal with it anymore and my mother truly thought he would kill me, so I left. My oldest brother left at age 29. They say he was drinking before losing control of his truck, crashing it into a tree and bouncing off and hitting another tree, before breaking his neck. My youngest brother is an alcoholic who began drinking at an early age, ignoring all of the signs. He went through three marriages and a multitude of jobs including the military, all ending in violence and disgrace. (Anonymous adult child of an alcoholic)

The following relates the irrational and destructive effects alcohol can have on the family:

I loved going to Susan's house in affluent Highlands Ranch where I could sit in her home theater and watch movies, or soak in her hot tub, or stare for hours into her salt water fish tank. Susan's father was a successful owner of a telecommunications company. One evening, I walked down stairs to get a glass of water. Susan's father barreled down the stairs in a drunken rage demanding that "I go back upstairs and never be seen wondering alone in the kitchen again!" He followed me up the stairs, and to punish Susan, he snatched the computer from her desk and threw it at her, sending her monitor crashing through the second story window on to the driveway below. Susan is now estranged from her alcoholic father and her mother who defended him. (An anonymous victim)

Another individual effected by the disease of alcoholism relates: Donna Smith was found dead in her apartment at the age of thirty-two. During one of her many drinking binges, her liver stopped working and her organs failed. Her family has never recovered from their loss. I never met Donna, but her absence will be heavily felt at my wedding as I marry her younger brother. Her absence is felt every day as her mother, father, and brother wonder why she died and what they could have done to save her.

The following is an intimate account of a life lost. This case was documented in the media:

One June 4th, 2005, I received a call from and old friend that Arlene Gavrilis, a high school classmate, had been killed by a drunk driver. She died on her wedding day. On June 28, 2005, my roommate and I went to dinner with her current love interest. He allured us with his southern charm, humored us with his quick wit, and impressed us with his genuine interest in humanity. Marty was a recent transplant to New York from Mississippi, working with an insurance company in the big city. On June 29th, Melissa wondered when she would see Marty again and how their relationship would progress. On July 1, Marty invited Melissa and I to a party. With no designated driver and no plans to stay the night, Marty had no intention of making good decisions but also had no intention to kill. With a blood alcohol of 0.28, Marty drove down the Meadowbrook Parkway. In a split second, Marty was transformed from a sweet, southern gentleman to a murderer. Two lives were lost as Marty slammed his pickup truck into a wedding limo, beheading a 7-year-old girl, and instantly killing the limo driver. He had no intention of spending the next eighteen years to life in prison, but the alcohol decided for him. The debate ensued in the media: Is Martin Heidgen a monster? Does he deserve a murder sentence? The jury believed that he did and the families of the innocent lives lost agreed. Marty was not a monster. He made a terrible, deadly, irreversible, life-changing decision. Sober, Marty was kind, loving, compassionate and responsible. Intoxicated, Marty became a murderer. Alcohol is a drug which clouded his judgment, altered his perception and robbed him of his clarity.

Denial and the progressive and illogical nature of the disease of alcoholism:

My cousin is an alcoholic and has been for many years. No one really believed he had a problem with alcohol or perhaps everyone just ignored this sad reality. It got to a point where John's alcoholism could no longer be covered up or denied. John was a handsome young man with many plans for the future. He was engaged to a wonderful girl and they were both very happy. For as long as I can remember, John had always been the life of the party, at any family function where he always had a drink in his hand. By the end of the gathering, John was either acting obnoxious or falling all over the place. His brother or other family members would always help him off the floor or into the bathroom. His girlfriend always seemed very uncomfortable. Soon she stopped accompanying him to family gatherings. John's problem with alcohol got much worse as the years went by. He began drinking a gallon of wine a night and would go to his construction job the next day intoxicated or hung over. John continued this behavior until he got fired. His girl friend could no longer cope with him and she broke of the engagement. John gained over forty pounds and even lost some of his teeth. He was no longer handsome and far from happy. It wasn't until he suffered a heart attack and the family gathered in the emergency room that everyone finally admitted to one another that John was an alcoholic. There were no other alcoholics in the family so no one could explain how or why this disease effected him. Doctors advised him to lose weight and stop drinking. Even this did not change his behavior towards alcohol. He had two more heart attacks and he continues to drink. He does not want any help because he does not believe he has a problem. His alcoholism has destroyed his life and devastated family and friends.

The Disease of Alcoholism:

I was first introduced to alcohol at an extremely young age. In fact, I first experienced alcohol even before I was old enough to walk. My aunt told me that my grandmother used to rub Johnny Walker Red scotch on my gums when I was teething as an infant. I was too young at that time, but as I now think about it, that distinct taste could have possibly been stored in my memory bank for future reference. I view alcoholism as a living entity that has unique powers. Alcoholism has patience and that is where its unique powers lie. At the age of fifteen, I began hanging out with the guys that were slightly older than I was, and to fit in, I indulged in what they did which was drink beer. This became a daily routine, and I did not have a clue that it was the beginning of what I later learned was an unhealthy addiction. Alcoholism is a progressive disease and because it was so cunning, I did not even realize that it took me no time at all to graduate from sharing a quart of beer with the guys to purchasing my own quart of beer after the game. At this point which was still early in my addiction, the alcoholism took flight. I found myself drinking beer as if it were soda. There was no need for my older friends or basketball; any excuse would do. During my sophomore and junior year in high school, I used to go to sleep drinking beer and wake up having beer for breakfast. After awhile the beer was ok, but it no longer had the same effect. I now know that my level of tolerance was progressing along with the disease. Back then the disease was too cunning for me to see that it was leading me on a journey that was impossible to find your way back. At the age of seventeen, I began to use hard alcohol. Drinking alcohol was normal for me because I grew up in an environment where everyone that I was surrounded by drank liquor. My entire family drank, from my grandmother who drank on a daily basis, to my mother who drank on the weekends. This is another example of how cunning the disease of alcoholism really is. Entire generations become addicted before anyone realizes what is going on. As time progressed so did the amount of hard liquor I consumed. Alcohol took over control of my body. My body had adapted to alcohol and without it, I just didn't feel comfortable. This pattern of drinking went on for years, as I progressively chose stronger and stronger alcohol. During this period, I also got sick after a night of heavy drinking, so I would try new drinks to see which one I could drink the most without getting sick in the morning. I now realize that there was not such a drink. The cunningness of the disease kept me in denial for a very long time. I never considered myself an alcoholic: Those were the bums that slept in cardboard boxes and wore dirty clothes. I had a job, a place to live, a girlfriend, and all of the things that normal people had. Besides, I could stop drinking anytime I wanted to. The baffling part of the disease of alcoholism was that no matter how many times that I stopped drinking, I could not stay stopped. There was always a reason to pick up a drink after a brief period of abstinence: A birthday party, a party, a ball game, a movie, it's payday, you mention it and it was, 'I'll drink to that.' My sister once called me an alcoholic and I looked at her like she was talking to the wrong person. I actually looked around to see if there was someone standing behind me.

In reality, I had been an alcoholic for quite some time; I just remained in deep denial. What my sister had said to me went in one ear and out the other. It did not dawn on me that the reason that my life was at a stagnant point and the reason why I could not keep a good job was a direct result of my drinking. I had become a 'functioning alcoholic,' which really does not exist. If one is an alcoholic, one is not really functioning. Alcohol distorts all sense of perception, therefore, what one thinks is not what it really is. Another really baffling reality of the disease of alcoholism is the fact that one has no control over alcohol. As humans, we are used to being in control of certain things. We learn this idea very early in life. I remember one particular incident that replays itself in my mind. It was when I made a conscious decision about how much alcohol I was going to drink one night. It was Friday night and I decided to do laundry, but of course I had to drink to entertain myself while waiting for the clothes to finish. Since it was a 24 hour laundry, I decided to catch the liquor store right before closing which was at 12 midnight. I bought one pint of liquor; that would be sufficient. Well that thought went right out the window. That first pint was gone before an hour had passed and now my disease had taken over. After a trip to the bootlegger and a second pint of liquor, I finally managed to finish the laundry, but my addiction was just getting started. What started out as a plan to have a limited amount of alcohol turned into a full fledged weekend binge over which I had no control. This part of the disease was extremely baffling being that I considered myself a take charge person. In reality it was the disease which was actually in charge. This type of behavior continued for a long time with me believing that someday I would find the right formula which would allow me to control my drinking. The insidious part of the disease lies in the fact that the alcohol has one doing things that one would not normally do. I consider myself to have good sense. I know it is not normal to have an Olde English 800 Malt Liquor for breakfast, but this is what the disease of alcoholism had me believe was normal. Alcohol had me in such a deep state of denial that I did not realize that at certain times while suffering from my disease I was actually homeless. It never dawned on me that if the individual with whom I was staying at the time asked me to leave I would have no place to go.

I remember something that I did while suffering from the disease of alcoholism that makes my skin crawl. During one of my drinking binges, I had been at one of my crash pads and fell asleep while drinking Wild Irish Rose wine. While I was asleep I had left the cap of the bottle off and some roaches had gotten into the wine. When I awoke the next morning and found the bottle full of roaches, I took a sock and strained the wine through it and drank it for breakfast without a second thought. After all of that, I was still in denial. The disease of alcoholism had robbed me of my spirit. (Anonymous recovering alcoholic)

CHAPTER 6: ALCOHOL IS A DRUG: DID YOU GET IT?

America: What's Wrong?

Vodka soaked tampons, funnels of alcohol channeled to the rectum, snorting Vodka, Vodka eyeballing, drinking hand sanitizers, inhaling alcohol, Vodka bongs, underage drinking, binge drinking, traffic fatalities, health care cost, alcohol and crime, police unaccountability, short and long term effects of alcoholism, the disease of alcoholism, America, wake up! One has just been enlightened to some pretty alarming trends and consequences as it relates to alcohol, the drug one does not even consider a drug!

Armed with all of this information, I fear that we have still not fathomed the destructive nature of our sick thinking as we continue to deceive ourselves as to the true nature of alcohol addiction. I am disgusted and saddened by the visual of a beautiful baby sitting at a bar with a glass of wine in her little hands as the bartender steadfastly serves patrons their favorite libation. On another page, two young children proudly look into a camera as they are captured drinking beverages amongst a bartender and drinkers. The pictures are depicted in a March 24, 2010, New York Post article titled, "Hey baby, come here often?" The article speaks to the growing trend for parents to bring their children to bars with them as they drink and socialize with other drinkers. The article quotes a mother who relates, "I used to be one of those moms who thought bars and kids didn't mix." You think!! She references her two children, "sitting pin straight atop a couple of stools dipping their fries into ketchup while our friend casually sipped a martini." The mother goes on to say, "For the past two weeks, I've been baby barhopping which is a great way to explore the city, especially when you are low on baby sitters." She goes as far as to recommend, "the best places to raise a glass while you are raising your kids." Sadly the Post reveals that the New York State Liquor Authority, permits such behavior as long as the child is with an adult and the bar does not object.

America, what's wrong? How can we be so blind to the destructive nature of our thinking. As surely as flowers bloom and die, we plant the seeds of destruction in our young as our choices and actions plant subliminal messages that perpetuate alcoholism.

We have the audacity to point fingers at "crack heads" and "dope fiends" as if they're the problem! As we naively are lulled into thinking, "it's just alcohol," our America is being killed physically, psychologically, and spiritually. How unhappy are we that we go through such great lengths to get high by totally disregarding the potentially fatal effects of our extreme behavior?

I am saddened by the harsh realities of the disease of alcoholism, and I am alarmed that we are more comfortable in our denial than with the truth. Something is missing: we have lost our spirit, our life force.

Prayer and Epitaph

I pray for all of the sick and suffering alcoholics whose lives have become completely unmanageable, who are lost and suffering in a hole of despair, trapped. I pray for the hundreds of thousands of children and mothers and fathers and significant others who are subjected to the emotional and physical ravage at the hands of alcoholism. How does one minimize their suffering and pain? I pray for all who continue to turn a blind eye and deaf ear to the realities of our dysfunctional relationship with alcohol. America, listen to the pleas; listen to the cries: Help me: I need your help.

RIP

From the Cradle to the Grave

Here lie the children who once were

Innocence lost

Spirits gone

*Succumb to the insidious disease
of denial and alcoholism*

CHAPTER 7: THE PHARMACEUTICAL INDUSTRY

Pablo Escobar, Scarface, Pharmaceutical Companies: The First One is Always Free

When one congers up notions of drug dealers, who does one think of? Of course, the reigning king of kings, the fictitious, but infamous Scarface: "Say hello to my little friend"; or maybe the real king, Pablo Escobar, "El Patron" of Columbia; or the newly appointed Joaquin "El Chapo" Guzman of Mexico, followed by any one of the other top ten international drug czars including: Amado Carrillo Fuentes, "Lord of the Skies" of Mexico, (business, cocaine), Khun Su "the Opium King" of Burma (business, heroin), Griselda Blanco, "the Black Widow" of the USA, (business, cocaine), Jose Gonzalo Rodriguez Gacha of Columbia, (business, cocaine), Carlos Lehder of the Bahamas, (business, cocaine), Felix Mitchell, "the Cat" of the USA, (business, crack, cocaine, heroin), Santiago Luis Polanco Rodriguez, "Yayo" of the USA, (business, crack), Paul Lir Alexander, "the Baron of cocaine," of Brazil, and Rick Ross, "Freeway," of the USA, (business, cocaine).

Stepping down a tier, one may think of the five Italian-American Mafia crime families, or maybe one thinks of Frank Lucas, a 1970's Harlem kingpin who ran a multi-million dollar enterprise trafficking drugs in the coffins of Vietnam soldiers. He was noteworthy because he by- passed the Mafia and established a direct link with Asia. Frank Lucas was recently portrayed by Denzel Washington in the film, <u>American Gangster</u>. One may remember Bumpy Johnson, portrayed by Moses Gunn in the 1971 film, <u>Shaft</u>,

Lawrence Fishburne in the 1997 film, <u>Hoodlum</u>, Clarence Williams III in the 2007 film, <u>American Gangster</u>. Maybe one thinks of "Nicky" Barnes, "Mr. Untouchable," a Harlem drug dealer in the 1970's, who modeled his African American crime organization, "the Council" after the Italian mob families. Maybe one thinks of Rayful Edmond, a notorious drug dealer who was instrumental in introducing crack into the Washington, D.C. area, or Frank Mathews, "Black Caesar," from North Carolina, intimately known by the DEA and responsible for the 1971 Atlantic Summit, including the major African American and Hispanic dealers across the United States whose primary purpose was to serve the Italian Mafia's control of heroin in the inner cities.

Drug production and distribution are one of the most profitable trades on any level, an enterprise to be reckoned with. Like any other business, "The first one is always free": A tactic that lures unsuspecting victims who falsely believe they are getting something for nothing: The ultimate beginning of a long and sometimes fatal relationship, where profit is the game, sometimes at the expense of human life. One can easily identify with the reality of the drug trade. It has been depicted and glamorized in movies, on TV shows, and even periodicals which shed light on the lucrative nature of the business. One may reference Forbes Magazine's inclusion of Mexican Drug Lord, Joaquin, "El Chapo" Guzman Loera as one of the world's billionaires.

So what does this have to do with pharmaceutical companies? Are you looking back at the title of the chapter in confusion? Are you wondering why pharmaceutical companies, infamous drug lords and notable drug dealers are paired in the same category? Well America, let's for one moment look at the essence of the pharmaceutical companies from another perspective - business, production and distribution of drugs. Primary purpose: Profit: By any means necessary, despite pre-existing knowledge of the dangers of drugs: Lives lost: Collateral damage. Are you beginning to see the parallel? I'm sure you are saying that the association is ludicrous and a gross oversimplification of the facts. Bare with me and consider the realities that may have escaped you.

Waiting For Your Primary Care Doctor. Pharmaceutical Suits and Primary Care Doctors

Have you noticed that the wait at your primary care doctor is getting longer and longer? Sometimes there are just a few patients ahead of you but twenty minutes turn into an hour and the next thing you know, a couple of hours have passed and patience turns into intolerance, which turns into anger, which culminates in rescheduling your appointment in order to meet your other commitments for the day. Poor timing? I think not! Have you noticed that during that long wait, several very attractive, well dressed, young men and women toting wheeled cases in one hand and coffee or donuts, or lunch, or other treats in the other: Umh? Who are these individuals who take precedence over you? It's the pharmaceutical representatives! Their job is to introduce all of the new medications to the doctors with the expectation that they will in turn, pass them on to their patients. Of course the perks, some of which we see and more extravagant ones such as dinner and even trips which we don't see are incentives for the doctors to promote these new medications. An ABC report indicates that, "Pharmaceutical companies spend over 2 billion sending doctors to more than 314,000 events every year" in order for them to promote the efficacy of new medications. Now it is finally your time to see the doctor. He examines you and prescribes a particular medication. You look at the prescription wondering, "How much is this one going to cost?" The doctor comes out with the ultimate surprise. He just happens to have some free samples just left by one of the pharmaceutical representatives. Of course you are elated at the prospects of saving a lot of money on prescription cost and in some way you naively believe that you have "gotten over" on the industry. Unfortunately, you are missing a couple of significant realities. Remember the business tactic of street dealers who peddle their drugs: "The first one is always free." That same business tactic is employed by the pharmaceutical companies. Although you were initially given free samples, they run out! The prescribed medication eventually must be filled over and over again, sometimes for years, sometimes for life. Secondly, and potentially more serious is the fact that these free samples are often part of a post marketing surveillance done by the pharmaceutical companies as part of FDA testing to ascertain the effectiveness and any potential side effects of the new medication. The FDA approval process can take up to ten years and ultimately, only one in five drugs is approved. In essence, America, we are all guinea pigs for the pharmaceutical companies. Consider the thousands of individuals who use any one of these drugs for any period of time in the interim of FDA testing. Consider the many drugs which are recalled because of potentially fatal side effects. Consider the hundreds of millions of dollars made by the pharmaceutical companies before the drug is removed from the market. Consider all of the drugs that have been recalled that are still accessible to the public: Collateral damage! It's all about the profit!

Direct to Consumer Advertising/America's Mantra: Immediate Gratification and Resolution

Another decisive tactic used by the pharmaceutical companies to promote their drugs is "direct to consumer advertising." One can barely get through their favorite television program, particularly during day time hours, without being inundated by commercials promoting new medications which promise anything and everything short of immortality. In an article by Linda Johnson for ABC.Com, (2002), "Drug company advertising aimed at ordinary people instead of doctors tripled in the United States between 1996 and 2000 to nearly 2.5 billion a year." It is important to look at trends from 1996 because it was in 1997 that the FDA began allowing the television to promote medications without specifying a long litany of side effects. They were required to reference an Internet address for more detailed information; however, Web information can be dubious. The (2002) article also indicates that, "The total spending of prescription drug promotions grew about 70% from 9.2 billion in 1996 to 15.7 billion in 2000." These expenditures continue to soar today as the public continues to be bombarded with drug advertisements. Pharmaceutical companies spend billions of dollars on advertising and promotion, almost twice as much as they spend on research. This form of advertisement undoubtedly, encourages the public to use particular drugs. Hence, the pharmaceutical companies continue to expend large amounts of money for advertisement of drugs which ultimately yield substantial profits in the end. Unsuspecting consumers armed with limited knowledge of the efficacy and side effects of a drug, visit their primary care doctors demanding that the most effective medication for their illness is the medication they have just learned about on TV. Doctors then spend more time trying to educate their patients as to the importance of individual assessments and individualized treatment which may in fact, not include the drug they have just encountered on TV. Unfortunately, many desperate Americans looking for a quick fix either find a doctor or go through some other possibly illegal channel to secure a medication which ultimately in the long run can have severe and even fatal side effects. Keep in mind that one medication can potentially save your life but that same medication in combination with other medications can be counterproductive. The reality is that millions of Americans are hospitalized each year as a result of side effects from medication. One may reference a (2003) medical report, "Death by Medicine," by Doctors, Gary Null, Carolyn Dean, Martin Feldman, and Debora Rasio which indicates that "106,000 deaths were attributed to prescription drugs." Reportedly, this is a conservative number. A further article by Jessica Fraser, Citizen Journalist (July 5, 2005), also wrote an article claiming that prescription drugs are 16,000% more deadly than terrorists. Referencing the tragedy of 911, she relates that over 750,000 people actually die in the US from modern medicine.

Who are these pharmaceutical companies? The following is a list of the twelve largest pharmaceutical companies ranked by revenues as of July 2009: (order and assets are finite):

Company Country Revenues (USD Millions)
Johnson & Johnson United States 63,747.0

Pfizer United States 48,296.0

GlaxoSmithKline United Kingdom 44,654.0

Roche Switzerland 44,267.5

Sanofi-Aventis France 42,179.0

Novartis Switzerland 41,459.0

AstraZeneca United Kingdom 31,601.0

Abbott Laboratories United States 29,527.6

Merck United States 23,850.3

Wyeth United States 22,833.9

Bristol-Myers-Squibb United States 21,366.0

Eli Lilly United States 20,378.0

Note: Reportedly, there is additional revenue as well as additional involvement in other industries which yield additional revenue. The reality is that the pharmaceutical industry is the most profitable industry, yielding multi-trillion dollar profits. Drug distribution on any level, whether it be illegal or legitimate is a profitable business: The term legitimate is used with caution.

Pharmaceutical companies are relentless in their ploys to promote new drugs and they can in fact be unscrupulous adapting an agenda of profit at the expense of human life. We can no more condemn them, however, than we can the illicit drug trade which provides all of the heroin to the "dope fiends" and the crack to the "crack heads." There are more Americans addicted to prescription drugs than all of the "dope fiends" and "crack heads" put together. It behooves us to point fingers at a specific population because they are us and their problem is our problem - different drug, same illness.

I have maintained on numerous occasions that we live in a drug addicted, chemically dependent society. Our insatiable need to get outside ourselves, to create an illusion of well being, and to fix what ever ails us will be our demise. Somehow, we have come to believe that there is a pill for every ailment and the solution to the side effects is to take another pill. The attitude of many Americans has disabled our natural ability to live life on life terms with the power and the spirit within us and we have "copped out" for an apparently easier solution. Immediate gratification and immediate resolution have become our mantra. Consequently, if we can't sleep, we take a pill; if we want to stay awake, we take a pill; if we are depressed, we take a pill; if we are hyper vigilant, we take a pill; if we are anxious, we take a pill; if we want to enhance our sex life, we take a pill, and if we are in any degree of pain, we take a pill. Not only does America have a pill for everything, we have a pill for a pill.

You Can't Sleep? There's a Pill for That.

Let's for a moment, take a look at the prescription sleeping pill industry. Remember, the focus is not only on the pharmaceutical companies but on the individuals who make choices. I premise this information with the fact that many Americans do suffer with legitimate sleeping disorders. Sleep is vital to our lives. During REM sleeping, in point, our brain and our body are rejuvenated comparable to the charge from a battery. Sleep deprivation can cause mood disorders and exacerbate a host of pre-existing conditions. In this regard, thank goodness the pharmaceutical companies provides us with medication that can potentially alleviate serious sleeping disorders. Thousands of Americans, however, who have not been diagnosed with a sleeping disorder have taken it upon themselves to medicate themselves with sleeping pills. It has been found that stress and factors such as the normal everyday pressures of life including jobs, family, finances, loss, for example, can have a profound impact on one's ability to have a restful sleep. There are specific strategies one can use to address inadequate sleeping patterns such as identifying the stress in your life, engage in relaxing activities before bedtime, i.e., a relaxing bath, warm milk or calming tea, avoid caffeine up to six hours before bedtime and alcohol up to two hours before bedtime, create a relaxing environment free of light and noise and other stimuli, and don't bring work into the bedroom; reserve the bed for sleeping. There are many techniques to enhance sleeping, but no, we would rather reach for that little sleeping pill which is an immediate solution to our problem.

Once again the pharmaceutical companies spare no expense at elaborate commercials which are so alluring you could possibly go to sleep just listening to the possibilities. They provide many choices in sleeping aids including Sonata, Ambien, or Ambien CR which is time released, Lunesta, Halcion, Rozeom, just to name a few. These sleeping aids are antihistamine based or they are a benzodiazepine which is a sedative hypnotic. In our zeal to go to sleep, I don't know if anyone bothers to listen to the warnings that accompany these drugs. They may not be safe for you if you have a history of drug abuse, depression, lung disease, liver or kidney disease, respiratory problems, or if you are pregnant or breast feeding. Most of them are habit forming and should be stopped gradually or withdrawal symptoms may incur including anxiety, nightmares, stomach and muscle cramps, nausea, vomiting, sweating, and shakiness. They may also interact with other medications you are taking, but they will make you go to sleep! Of course, many of them are ineffective after taking them for two weeks.

One also has the option of taking over the counter sleeping aids such as Unisom, Nytol, and Sominex; just to name a few. Most of these medications contain an antihistamine which is used in the treatment of allergy symptoms but their side effect is drowsiness. Like their prescription counterparts, over the counter sleeping aids can also have side effects including but not limited to drowsiness, dizziness, reduced mental alertness, poor coordination, constipation and dry mouth and throat: But you sleep!

A growing trend today, particularly among college students and young adults is to take sleeping aids in combination with pain relievers including Anacin P.M., Excedrin P.M., and the almighty Tylenol P.M.

Do You Need to Stay Awake? There's a Pill for That.

If sleeping is not a problem and one would like to stay awake, there is a pill for that! They are particularly alluring to students who have to stay awake cramming for exams and writing papers, truck drivers who drive long distances, people who work over night and people who are doing double shifts. Some of these medications are Alert, NoDoz, Stay Awake, and Vivarin. They are basically no more than caffeine tablets. Caffeine is a stimulant commonly found in your coffee, tea, soda, chocolate, etc. Caffeine is a central nervous system stimulant which speeds up your central nervous system and allows you to remain alert and awake. According to Medicine Net.Com, you should tell your doctor if you have heart disease, diabetes, anxiety disorders, depression, ulcers or allergies. Of course you should not take it if you are pregnant or nursing. Side effects may include nausea, stomach upset, insomnia, restlessness, nervousness, tremors, headaches, dizziness, rapid breathing, chest pain, confusion or fatigue. Withdrawal may include headache, anxiety, and muscle tension.

Amphetamine based pills are a stronger alternative for those Americans who find the other options ineffective. Amphetamines are powerful and toxic central nervous system stimulants which must be prescribed by the doctor. Ironically, amphetamines are a popular alternative for doctors who sometimes spend long hours in the hospital and airplane pilots who fly long distances. They are however, very popular among the general public and one sometimes go to great lengths securing them in unconventional ways.

Are You Depressed? There's A Pill for That.

Taking a pill has become a normal reactive mechanism for dealing with life on life terms. Consequently, whenever we feel the slightest degree of sadness or depression, a pill is a quick fix. Being depressed and suffering from depression are on opposite ends of the spectrum. Depression is an imbalance of brain chemicals called neurotransmitters. The National Institute of Mental Health indicates that depression is the leading disability in the United States. 18.8 Million Americans are suffering with depression at any given moment and women are twice as likely to suffer with depression as compared with their male counterparts. Signs off depression are sadness, excessive crying, loss of interest, poor contemplation, feelings of worthlessness and helplessness, lack of energy, change in sleeping patterns and appetite, and weight loss. If one experiences five or more of these symptoms for longer than two weeks, it is recommended that they see a doctor who will more than likely prescribe an antidepressant medication. If one is in need of an antidepressant medication, there are many from which to choose. They all work by altering the neurotransmitters: Serotonin, dopamine, and norepinephrine which are the main chemicals involved in depression and effect mood, alertness and energy. They include but are not limited to Selective Serotonin Reuptake Inhibitors (SSRIs) which act on the neurotransmitter, Serotonin, and is generally used for individuals over the age of 18 who suffer from minor depressive illness or early stage depression. SSRIs include the familiar Prozac, which lingers longer in the body before it is totally excreted, Lexapro, Celexa, Luvox, Paxil and Zoloft. A second category of antidepressants are called Tricyclic Antidepressants which increase the brains supply of Serotonin and Norepinephrine. They include Elavil, Norpramin, Tofranil and Aventyl. A third category of antidepressants are Monamine Oxidase Inhibitors (MAOIs). They effect the neurotransmitters Serotonin, Norepinephrine and Dopamine. Normally, once these chemicals do their job in the brain, they get burned up by a protein in the brain called Monamine Oxidase which is a liver and brain enzyme. Monamine Oxidase Inhibitors (anti depressants) prevent the break down so that the neurotransmitters pile up in the brain. Since depression is associated with low levels of neurotransmitters, the pile up or increase effects depression. Unfortunately, these MAOIs effect other neurotransmitters, which in turn have an effect on what ever that neurotransmitter is responsible for regulating; for example blood pressure is elevated. Individuals who have heart problems, epilepsy, bronchitis, asthma and high blood pressure are cautioned against taking these drugs. A forth category of antidepressants are Serotonin-Norepinephrine Reuptake Inhibitors (SNRIs). These are a new class of antidepressant that treats major depressive disorders. They include Cymbalta, Pristig and Effexor which can also treat anxiety disorders, panic disorders and social anxiety disorders which can accompany depression.

If all of these anti-depressants are not effective, there is Abilify which can augment the anti-depressants one is already taking.

We are inundated with anti-depressant drugs. Thank goodness we have them. Depression is a very serious disorder that can be fatal. We are fortunate to have medications which treat the disease and potentially enhance one's quality of life and overall functioning. The problem, however, continues to resonate in our attitude. Even in the case of clinical depression certain variables must be considered. Firstly, it is important to note that the antidepressant medications are not a cure in and of themselves. They are designed to relieve the symptoms of depression and as such the medication should be used in conjunction with therapy. Secondly, one must consider that all medications have side effects specifically, side effects of anti- depressant medication may include but are not limited to dry mouth, headache, nausea, anxiety, nervousness, dizziness, weight gain, insomnia, difficulty urinating, sexual dysfunctions, blurred vision, heart problems, and ironically depression and suicide. In some instances as in the case with MAOIs there are some dietary restrictions in that certain foods interact with these drugs, thereby affecting their efficacy. The anti-deprssant Paxil has also been linked to birth defects. These important variables must be explored between the patient and the doctor along with an informative discussion as to the benefits of the drug in comparison to the risk. Therefore, the combination of medication, therapy and education are paramount in the treatment of depression.

America, however, is still faced with a dilemma. What happens to all of the individuals who are not suffering with clinical depression who are faced with life challenges and believe that any level of distress or depression requires a pill. It has been established that being depressed and suffering from depression are quite different. It is quite normal for one to experience times or episodes of feeling down or sad. It is very normal for an individual to experience a range of different feelings. Work can be overwhelming, the demands of school can be stressful, the balance of role relationships can be demanding, divorce can turn our world up side down, loss can leave a deep void which impacts upon our emotional well being and is very difficult to process, and one is faced with debilitating illnesses. Sometimes the pain of living life on life terms is so great, we would like to become an ostrich and submerge our heads in a hole. We may in fact experience many of the symptoms associated with clinical depression. The real task is to learn the coping strategies we need to deal with and process all of the challenges life brings. Establishing and relying on supports, setting priorities, focusing on our spiritual and physical self, getting proper amounts of sleep, exercising, eating nutritionally, and avoiding mind altering drugs, including alcohol, are viable tools in dealing with the depression brought on by just living life.

But of course that is too difficult. We don't want to do the work. It is so much easier reaching for the pill that's going to make it all better. Antidepressants are designed for individuals suffering from depression, not individuals who are burdened with life. One must remember that antidepressants alter our brain chemistry. They are not to be taken lightly, America. The inclination for us to take a pill and the tendency for doctors to prescribe anti-depressants without a thorough assessment and diagnosis and without a referral to a support system is a grave injustice to our well being. The solution is not in a pill.

Do You Want a Cheap High? Need to Focus: Pass the Class: Get the Job Done? There's a Pill for That.

What do "crack heads," "dope fiends," high school and college students, medical students, professionals, parents, and you and I have in common? Far too many of us use and abuse drugs for non medical purposes: Specifically, the illegal use of prescription medications that are used to treat Attention Deficit Hyperactivity Disorder, (ADHD). Who do we blame? Is it the pharmaceutical companies who profit from the vast revenues generated from our diseased attitude, a society that perpetuates the notion that mind altering substances are a solution for living your best life, or Americans who fall prey to the insidious attitudes, but at the same time must be held accountable for their choices and the consequences there of? I sometimes believe that there is a general conspiracy in our society as it relates to our dysfunctional relationship to drugs. Perhaps, if we continue to focus on the "crack heads" and "dope fiends" we will remain oblivious to the true nature and implications of our own behavior.

America, we are faced with two dilemmas: The first is the misdiagnosing and over diagnosing of Attention Deficit Hyperactivity Disorder (ADHD) of our children with the drug protocol of amphetamine based drugs and the second is the misuse and abuse of these medications among individuals who have not been diagnosed with ADHD.

Something is wrong with a society which has lost perspective on the worth, value, and diversity of our youth. In our zest to resolve any level of dysfunction with a pill, a grave injustice has been rendered to our children. We inundate them with elaborate marketing ploys that promise a cure in a pill; we medicate them with no consideration of the side effects of certain medications; we quiet their enthusiasm, their creativity and their ingenuity which ultimately stifles their true potential. Why? Because sometimes a quiet youngster is just simply easier to deal with than one who is demanding or inquisitive. Our children live in a complex world. They are confronted with challenges that rival their adult counterparts. Whether one comes from a nurturing and supportive environment, or a chaotic, dysfunctional and abusive one, the transition from home to school, the separation from the familiar parent, the introduction to a new social group, is a challenging experience that is processed in unique ways by each child. How did we come to believe that all children must adhere to structure and behave in the same way at all times and in all situations? Many children act out particularly in school as a vehicle of communication. At any given time children can be overactive, impulsive and inattentive, so you work with them as they need special consideration and nurturing. Class rooms, however, are traditionally over crowded and the teacher/student ratio is not always conducive to an enriching learning environment. Our children become victim to a system which labels them because they are energetic and stimulated beyond our degree of comfortability. Perhaps we should focus more on teacher training and parental skill building. Unfortunately, the focus is on the unruly child which is distracting the entire class. Consequently, the teacher makes a referral to the school psychologist; the child is evaluated, and far too often diagnosed with ADHD and prescribed medication. The child returns to class, medicated, and generally, the teacher's only concern is that the child is no longer disruptive. Furthermore, usually the child is a male given the reality that boys are disproportionately diagnosed with ADHD than females. Health care professionals are over zealous to say the least, in diagnosing children with ADHD. A child who misbehaves in school does not necessarily have ADHD.

Far too many of our nation's children are being misdiagnosed with the disorder and the over- prescribing of medications such as Ritalin, has hit an all time high. The over diagnosing and over prescribing of prescription medication for ADHD is alarming. Furthermore, the stark reality is that there is limited medical research which addresses the long term consequences of the treatment protocol particularly on very young children.

For clarity, just as in the case of depression, one is in no way minimizing the severity of ADHD. When diagnosed properly, it is a very serious disorder that affects 3%-5% of school age children. Of course adolescents and adults are also diagnosed with the disorder. As common and widespread as ADHD is, it is a mysterious disorder in terms of what causes it. There is some consensus among health care professionals that it is a neurological or a neurobiological disease which may be attributed to an imbalance or deficiency in neurotransmitters. Other medical professionals believe that it may be genetic or environmental, a possible result of a brain injury, or a nutritional deficiency, or a reaction of sugar or food additives. Furthermore, there is no single test to determine ADHD. A thorough assessment must be done by a qualified license health professional. The assessment should include observation, family history, medical history, psychological testing measuring IQ and social and emotional adjustment, interviews with parents and teachers to assess behavior and a physical exam to rule out any other medical conditions which may be effecting behavior. Symptoms of ADHD include inattention, hyperactivity and impulsivity; however, children with ADHD are not all the same and each child falls on different points of the spectrum. Some may be more inattentive falling on the attention deficit side where they are easily distracted and have a hard time focusing, may get bored very easily, may have difficulty completing assignments, or they may often daydream. Some children may experience more hyperactivity where they talk a lot or are very frigid; they may have difficulty sitting and they might dash from place to place. Other children may be impulsive; where there is limited delayed gratification, they are inpatient and they blurt out. Some children may have combined symptoms of the disorder. Each child is unique and each child requires an individualized treatment plan.

The drug protocol has traditionally been treatment with an amphetamine based drug. Although amphetamines are stimulants there is a paradoxical effect in children with ADHD: Instead of stimulating them, the medication has a reverse effect where they are generally calmer and able to focus and stick to task. One of the first and most popular medications is Ritalin. There is also Ritalin SR and Ritalin LA for extended release and long lasting consecutively. Other prescribed medications may be Adderall, Concerta, Dexedrine, Dextrostat, Stattera, and the new transdermal (patch) medication, Daytrana. Adderall, Dexedrine and Dextrostat are unique because they are recommended for children three years old or above. The remaining medications are recommended for children six years old and above, very young, to say the least. As with all medications, one must consider the side effects which may include: reduced appetite, headache, irritability, sleep problems, gastrointestinal upset, depression, anxiety, increased blood pressure, tics, which are repetitive movements, paranoia, and withdrawal. One must remember that psychotropic medications are not a cure. They are designed to manage the symptoms. They must be monitored by a psychiatrist and they should be given in conjunction with therapy and education by a qualified, licensed, health care professional.

The therapeutic value of medication for ADHD goes without question. The degree to which we misdiagnose and consequently prescribe psychotropic medications remain an area of grave concern that we must re-evaluate. The formulation of a more accurate and productive measure for dealing with our children must take precedence over control and profit.

As the overuse of these amphetamine based drugs proliferate our culture as a viable treatment for ADHD, conjointly, there is a rise in the abuse of these same medications by individuals who have not been diagnosed with ADHD. Here lies our second dilemma. According to the Drug Intelligence Center, a component of the U.S. Justice Department, Ritalin and other amphetamines are Schedule II substances as classified by the Control Substance Act. Other drugs included in this category are cocaine and methamphetamines. Drugs scheduled under Schedule II have a high potential for abuse and they may lead to psychological and physiological dependence. According to the Drug Enforcement Agency (DEA), there is an increase in abuse of these drugs by anyone from health care professionals to street addicts. Adolescents, high school and college students, medical students, and parents of children with ADHD have swelled the numbers of individuals abusing the drugs commonly prescribed for ADHD. The effects of these amphetamine based drugs on individuals who do not have ADHD are similar to cocaine, but they are substantially cheaper, ranging anywhere from .50 to $5.00 per pill. They are obtained easily from friends, dealers, stolen from children who have been prescribed the medication for ADHD, or the Internet where there are sites where no prescription is needed. These pills are alluring because they allow you to stay awake, stay focused, get all of your studying done, reduce appetite, create a feeling of euphoria and they are inexpensive. Common street names for these ADHD drugs are "Kiddie Cocaine,""Vitamin R," "R-Bull," "Smart Drug," "Kibbles & Bits," "Pineapple," "Skippy," etc.

Adderall, known by college students as the "magic pill," like Ritalin, is a very popular drug used by college students who are under a great degree of pressure from parents and a society who expects them to succeed. Adderall was originally introduced in the 60's under the name of Obetrol as a diet drug. It was banned by the Food and Drug Administration ten years after production; however, the pharmaceutical companies being the ingénues, maniacal entities that they are, re-introduced it in 1997 as Adderall for ADHD. Reportedly, it was "safer and more effective" than Ritalin. According to Mercy College's student Newspaper, The Impact (March 2010), Adderall is a "golden prescription," a gift from the prescription gods to students all over." The newspaper further indicates that "14% of campuses have abused some form of ADHD drugs including Adderall." The number increases to "25% among highly competitive schools." Reportedly, "Adderall is equivalent to prescription speed, and college campuses including Mercy become Adderall havens as a wide range of students use the pill to study."

An alarming reality is the manner in which individuals are taking these medications. Of course many take them the traditional route; however, many take the pill, chop it up and snort it thereby maximizing its potency and accelerating its action. One may remember that snorting drugs is a fast route of administration in that it skips the digestive process and enters the blood stream. A second and even more dangerous trend is to chop up the pill, add some water and inject it in your veins with a hypodermic needle. There are significant complications in shooting the drug because the fillers that bind the active ingredient in all pills are not necessarily bio-degradable. In other words, they are not water soluble. Consequently, when you inject the solution into your blood stream, those extraneous particles can block very small blood vessels which in turn, can damage your body such as your lungs or even the retina of your eyes. Of course addiction is another variable which has a profound impact on one's physiological, psychological and spiritual well being. Nevertheless, Americans continue to engage in this risky behavior all for the sake of immediate gratification. America, who's the addict?

Are You In Pain? Do You Have a Headache, or Toothache? Does Your Shoulder, Hip, Knee or Back Hurt? Are You Experiencing Any Discomfort? There's a Pill For That.

Mental anguish: Physical pain is a reality grounded in one's mind, whether real or imagined. How natural is one's inclination to ease suffering.

How easy is it to reach for that pill: The answer to all our prayers: That magic bullet that can take it all away and put one in a state of ease. Pain medication: A medical necessity: Pharmaceutical companies produce them: Americans abuse them.

Starting with simple over the counter pain relievers: Tylenol, Motrin, Advil, Aleve, Excedrin, Anacin, aspirin: What's your fancy? One has an idea about which works and which does not. I'm reminded by an early morning call for relief. 2 am: Nothing stirring: everyone sound asleep: The streets are still. Without a second thought, I quietly rise, dress and exit my home to my car. I proceed to drive a few short blocks to the 24 Hour Store to purchase a .50 pack of Anacin. I return home and with anticipation of relief, I take the pills and lie down quietly knowing that when I rise, the pills would have surely vanished any signs of pain or discomfort. Did it work? Of course.

How many times has one experienced a similar scenario? Let's for a moment play the tape back. An alternative to that midnight run was to explore any unrest or stress one may have been experiencing: Processing it: Putting it in perspective: Maybe one could have done some relaxation exercises to calm the body and the mind. . Maybe the headache was caused from dehydration as sometimes they are and a glass of water would have sufficed. But no, I chose the path of least resistance, at least in my mind. The action I had taken so many times before; I reached for the pill, the ultimate solution to all our problems.

If one is thinking: "Big deal, it was just a pill. It's not like I took a drink or got high! What's the problem?" Well America, Just as we have maintained all along, "It's not the pill," "It's not the behavior," "It's the attitude." There is always something outside of "self" that can make one feel better. And like any other addiction, it is illogical and irrational: 2am, driven by the need for relief. Whether I went to the store for an aspirin or I went to "Flako" (the drug dealer), it is the same attitude that drives one to feel comfortable or at ease, by any means necessary.

I wish our drug problem was as easy as removing the "crack heads" and "dope fiends." One must remember, the same attitude that defines an individual as a "crack head" or a "dope fiend" is the same attitude that defines the destructive drug taking behavior that far too many Americans engage in.

As easy as it was for me to go out at 2am to acquire my drug of choice is as easy as it is for some to procure all of the opiate pain killers, the other end of the spectrum; either to alleviate pain or because our drive to maintain an addiction is as strong as our natural desire to live. If we combined all of the "crack heads" and all of the "dope fiends" together, they would not equal the amount of Americans that abuse opiate pain medication. As reported in an article in the New York Times (June 14, 2008), "A Florida medical examiner found that the deaths caused by prescription drugs was three times the rates caused by all illicit drugs combined." "The Florida report analyzed 168,900 deaths state wide. Cocaine, heroin and methamphetamines caused 989 deaths; legal opiates - strong painkillers in brand name drugs like Vicodin and Oxycontin caused 2,328." Reportedly, the Federal Drug Enforcement agency similarly found that "Roughly seven million Americans are abusing prescription drugs. That would be an increase of 80% in six years and more than the total abusing cocaine, heroin, hallucinogens, ecstasy and inhalants." According to the TEDS Report (July 15, 2010) published by Substance Abuse and Mental Health Services Administration (SAMHSA), "The proportion of all substances abuse treatment admissions age 12 or older that reported any pain reliever abuse increased more than fourfold between 1998 and 2008, from 2.2 to 9.8 percent." The report further indicates that, "The increase in percentages of admissions reporting pain reliever abuse cut across age, gender, race/ethnicity, education, employment and region."

America, we have a problem. How long are we going to conveniently point fingers at the "crack heads" and the "dope fiends", as the crux of our problem? When do we start taking responsibility for our drug taking destructive behavior? How long do we continue to be lulled into a false sense of denial ("don't even no I am lying"); thinking because it is prescription opiates, prescribed by a doctor that some way that is different than procuring it from "Flako." Opiates are opiates, heroin is an opiate, prescription pain pills are opiates, drugs are drugs and addicts are addicts.

Unscrupulous doctors, you are part of America and part of the problem: Those of you who continually write prescription opiate painkillers exceeding the recommended dosage to individuals who are known addicts. What happened to the Hippocratic Oath, "To do no harm?" What happened to those ethics and values? Where is the accountability? One may reference the incidence of 2012 felony charges for doctors selling opiate painkillers extending from New York to Kentucky to Malibu. What purpose, whose purpose, does it serve when doctors enable addicts to continue with their self destructive and potentially fatal behavior: addicts who have no control because of their addiction; those who must secure these drugs by any means necessary in order to avoid the uncomfortabillity and sickness of withdrawal.

Street dealers, you are part of America and part of the problem. Under the guise of supply and demand, you peddle these opiate pain killers to sick addicts with no regard for their well being, with profit as your chief incentive.

Some senators and legislators don't see fit to allocate resources which will institute a tracking system which will restrict the dispensing of opiate pain medication in Florida that is notoriously becoming the "pill mill" state of America. The profusion of "pill mills" throughout America, but particularly in Florida, has greatly contributed to the prescription pain medication epidemic. "Pill Mills" are store front prescription clinics which profess, "Dispensing on site" of powerful pain killers and other psychotropic medications. One does not have to be a doctor to run them and, ironically, sometimes there is not even a doctor on site. Nevertheless, every day, all day, thousands of people from near and far flood these sites to fill prescription medications which have no restrictions on frequency or amount. As reported in the Miami Herald (8/14/10), "Local detectives say dispensing 240 tablets of Oxycodone and 100 tablets of Xanax per person is typical at some Tampa clinics." Reportedly, Tampa Florida has recently become the "epicenter of the states 'pill mill' problem." Tampa just surpassed Broward County and as reported by the Time, "has more pain clinics than burger franchises." The

<u>Time</u> further reports that "South Florida has 176 pill mills up from just 66 just 14 months before. Pill shopping trips to the Sunshine State are as common as Disney Vacation Holidays." "Pill mills" can exist, as previously stated, because there is no national tracking system to prevent the distribution of pill prescriptions. A data base would at least have to provide information on the dispensing of controlled medication which would ultimately restrict the allocation of prescription medication. In the meantime, the death rate from prescription drug overdose continues to escalate far surpassing cocaine and heroin. As reported in the Time, "Cocaine is no longer king in South Florida as it was during the Miami Vice era. Prescription Oxycodone now reigns supreme." America, dare you still point the finger?

Do You Want to Lose Weight? There's a Pill For That!

Americans beware. We are being exploited by pharmaceutical companies who market diet pills and prosper from the pain and misery of millions of Americans who suffer from a negative self image and life threatening eating disorders.

Food is as secure as a mother's womb, as sensuous as an orgasm; for some, it is one's most intimate relationship. We continually reach back to that place: Unmet needs, unresolved issues, insatiable desire for total anonymity, whether we want it or not. Dare anyone discover our secret: No control, no sense of self. Ultimately, one reverts back to what one knows: Food: Self destructive behavior. One is reminded that it's not about the food, or the drug, or the behavior. It's about acceptance or lack there of: the approval we yearn for, acceptance of self we have yet to acquire. One is going through the process of change: One is a work in transition. In the meantime, one escapes into the insanity of one's own despair. One, and 8 million others who have eating disorders: 7 million of which are women, and 1 million of which are men. How does one feel so isolated amongst so many? Sadly, our nation's children and young adults suffer the most. Reportedly, 95% of those who have eating disorders are between 12 and

25 years old. Consider information from the South Carolina Department of Mental Health. Reportedly, "50% of girls between the ages of 11 and 13 years old see themselves as overweight. 80% of 13 year olds have attempted to lose weight. The rate of minorities with eating disorders is similar to those of white women. 74% of American Indian girls reported dieting and purging with diet pills." Essence Magazine in 1994 reported "53% of their respondents, African American females were at risk of an eating disorder." In addition, eating disorders have the highest mortality rate of any other mental illness. A study by the National Association of Anorexia Nervosa indicates, "5-10% of anorexics die within 10 years, 18-20% will be dead after 20 years and only 30-40% ever fully recover."

Wouldn't it be great if we lived in a culture that glorified voluptuous hips and a large derriere, but we don't. The American standard of beauty, which is culturally determined, creates a very unrealistic picture of what beauty actually is. Individuals go to great lengths to achieve that standard, measuring their own reality against the expectations of others. Acceptance, rejection: We strive for that perfect self image. As long as we strive for external standards of beauty, we will never be beautiful. So we starve ourselves (Anorexia) and we binge and purge, (Bulimia) all for that elusive image; but until we own it, it will never be ours.

From the gut of our insecurities, from the essence of our despair, the pharmaceutical companies promise a solution in a pill. Diet pills that offer "amazing results," pills containing "herbal and natural ingredients," "advanced ingredients," "maximum strength," "money back guarantee:" That magic bullet that will have you looking like a Victoria Secret model. Isn't it ironic, that many of those models we aspire to be like, are subjected to the same unrealistic standards of American culture and fall prey to the insidious ploys of the diet industry? (We hear you Tyra Banks.)

The pharmaceutical companies have spared no expense. America is inundated with the hopes and dreams of being that perfect size. One sees the advertisements on TV; one hears them on the radio; stores and supermarkets are compensated for displaying weight loss products in visible locations and the Internet will research which products are the most popular and which promise the ideal body shape. Americans become unsuspecting victims who fall prey to the hype.

In a "nut shell," pharmaceutical companies offer three types of diet pills. One type is an appetite suppressant. One may remember that the way some drugs work is by their action on neurotransmitters. By increasing Serotonin or Catecholamine, two chemicals that effect mood and appetite, the body is tricked into believing it is not hungry or that it is full. The diet pill, Meridia, is a popular appetite suppressant. One may also remember Redux, a combination of Phentermine and Fenfluramine, otherwise known as the "Phen-Fen," which was withdrawn from the market in 1997 after several reports of damage to the heart valves, stroke and heart attack. Ironically, it was originally marketed as a "miracle drug."

Fat absorption inhibitors are a second type of diet pill. They prevent the body from breaking down or absorbing fat. The unabsorbed fat is eliminated with bowel movements. An example of a fat absorption drug is Xenical which blocks 30% of fat from being absorbed. Xenical is currently being sold over the counter as the popular Alli.

A third type of diet pill accelerates the body's metabolism. This is particularly popular among men. Following is a list of some of the most popular diet pills: Apidexin: Proved to deliver fast results and contains 8 clinically proven weight loss ingredients; Fenphedra which suppresses appetite and gives you a "happy feeling" and a feeling of well being caused by a combination of stimulants and Humulus Lupus(one of the only two plants in the family Cannabin Aceae; the other being marijuana; Lipovox which boast 10 highly concentrated extracts from 10 super foods; Testoripped which is a libido enhancing product and the favorate choice for guys who want to shed weight and build lean muscle; Adipozin-P, one of the newest appetite suppressants; Adipozin which boast 57% more weight loss than the leading diet pill and contains 9 clinically proven weight loss ingredients; 7 Day Detox and Lipovex Hardcore Detox which are detoxification supplements; 72 Hour Diet Pill which promises you can lose 12 pounds in 72 hours;

Liporexall which is "safe, effective and works," and Dieters Cheating Caps which blocks fat and suppresses the appetite.

Most diet pills are controlled substances which means that the doctors have restrictions on writing prescriptions for them because they are addictive. Xenical is an exception. In addition, the FDA has approved weight loss medications for short term use. Xenical and Meridia are the only drugs which have been approved for long term use, not to exceed two years.

Do the bennefits outweigh the risk? "Hell no." However, in one's quest for the ultimate body image, the high risk and consequences of these drugs are minimized. One must remember the illogical and irrational addictive attitude: It is far more important to be beautiful than it is to be healthy. I'm being factitious to make a point. Do the pharmaceutical companies stop to consider the risk? No. Consider some of the side effects of diet medications. They include, but are not limited to, increased heart rate, increased blood pressure, stroke, heart attack, dry mouth, sweating, constipation, insomnia, excessive thirst, light headedness, drowsiness, headache, anxiety, abdominal cramping, gas, leakage, oily stools, increased bowel movement, and inability to control bowels. One should inform the doctor if they have high blood pressure, heart disease, epilepsy, kidney disease, glaucoma, overactive thyroid, depression, a history of drug abuse and if they are breast feeding since birth defects have been detected in at least one mother who took diet pills while she was pregnant.

Drug Recalls

The pharmaceutical companies' blatant disregard for the health and well being of the American consumer is not only reflected in living risks but in the fatalities. There is no other industry that has sustained as many drug recalls as the diet industry. As reported in an article by Tom Castello, NBC, the FDA warns: "Stop Hydroxycut use now. The popular supplement is linked to reports of liver damage and at least one death." Reportedly 9 million packages have been sold last year." Dr Linda Katz of the FDA's

Nutrition Division relates, "23 reports of liver problems including death of a 19 year old boy." In addition, according to Medical News Today (December 23, 08), the FDA is seeking recall of 25 weight loss pills with potentially unsafe ingredients. Some of them include:

Joyful Slim Herbal Supplement
Slim-30 Herb Supplement
7 Day Herbal Slim
8 Factor Diet
7 Day/Night Formula
999 Fitness Essence
Extrim Plus
AMP
Imelda Perfect Slim
Perfect Slim
Perfect Slim 5X
Phyto Shape
Pro Slim Plus
Royal Slimming Formula
Slim 3 in 1
Slim Express 360
Slim Tech
Somotrim
Super Slim
Tripple Slim
Zhen de Shou
Fat Loss Slimming
2 Day Diet
3X Slimming Power
Japan Lingzhi 24 Hours Diet
5X Imelda Perfect Slimming
3 Day Diet.

Reportedly, these drugs contain undeclared pharmaceutical ingredients which put the consumer at risk. Some of the ingredients named are Sibutramine, which causes high blood pressure, seizures and heart attacks; Rimonabant, which has been linked to an increase in depression and suicidal thoughts; Phenytoin, an anti seizure drug and Phenolphthalein, which is a carcinogen used to test acidity in chemical experiments. Unfortunately, these are not the only diet medications which the FDA has recalled. When one considers that upwards of 45 million Americans take these diet supplements, the practice of marketing poison to Americans who suffer from eating disorders and negative self image is an atrocity.

Unfortunately, drug recalls are not restricted to the diet industry. Parija Kavilanz, a senior writer for CNN Money, cites an FDA report indicating that there were more than 1,742 drug recalls in 2009, exploding from the 426 reported in 2008. One may remember the largest children's recall in history when McNeil Consumer Healthcare, a subsidiary of Johnson & Johnson, reluctantly pulled their children's Tylenol, Motrin, Benadryl and Zyrtec off of the shelves. It was alleged that they tried to do damage control by secretly going store by store and quietly buying them back. Note, that this recall followed a 1982 Tylenol catastrophe when seven people died from ingesting Extra Strength Tylenol laced with cyanide. Another very popular drug recall one may remember is Vioxx, marketed in more than 80 countries by Merck & Company for arthritis.

Launched in 1999, Vioxx was used by more than two million people before it was removed from the market on September 30, 04 because of the risk of heart attack and stroke. Bextra, a similar COX-2 selective-non-steroidal anti-inflammatory drug was also recalled by the FDA on 4/7/05 for similar cardio-vascular risk. Ironically, Celebrex, also under Pfizer, continues to be marketed despite the fact that it is from the same class of drugs and poses the same kinds of risk. One may also remember the PPA scare in 2000. PPA is a common ingredient in many of our cold and diet medications some of which are Robitussin, Dimetapp, Contac, Triaminic, Comtrex, Tavist-D, Acutrim, and Dexatrim. As reported by CNN, the "FDA accepted findings in a Yale

University study that suggested PPA could be linked to between 200 and 500 hemorrhagic strokes annually." (CNN.Com-Health-FDA to Seek Removal of Several Cold, Diet Drugs From Stores, November, 2000.) Because of aggressive advertising, I am sure many of our younger readers remember YAZ, the birth control pill manufactured by Bayer. Yaz was recalled by the FDA in November, 2009 for poor manufacturing and quality control issues. Specifically, Bayer was accused of improper averaging of test results rather than reporting the results from each batch. In addition, there are several pending law suits against Bayer for serious side effects including but not limited to heart attack, stroke, blood clots, deep vein thrombosis, pulmonary disorders, etc. Pfizer, Inc.' equally aggressive ad campaign for Chantix is also probably quite familiar to many consumers. Chantix, a non-nicotine prescription medication targets nicotine receptors in the brain and acts as an antagonist, blocking nicotine from reaching them. In July 2009, the FDA issued a "Black Box Warning," mandating Pfizer to conduct further clinical trials that would determine the severity of reported side effects including, but not limited to, nausea, depression, anxiety, agitation, and suicide. In the interim, it is important to note that Chantix has been used by more than 4 million consumers.

Drug recalls abound. There are far too many to list and actually an entire text should be devoted to the improprieties as it relates to the pharmaceutical industry. According to Fox News, (June 5, 2012), "US drug recalls are common, not well publicized and they occur once every month.)" In addition, Dr. John Braithwaite, a former research criminologist and trade practice commissioner, speaks to the bribery, corruption and fraud in the testing of drugs. Reportedly, the pharmaceutical industry has the worst record of law breaking than any other industry. Dr. Braithwaite relates, "It is easy for the drug companies to arrange clinical trials by approaching sympathetic clinicians to produce the desired result that would assist the intended application of the drug. The incentive for clinical investigators to fabricate data is enormous. As much as $1,000 per subject is paid by American companies which enables some doctors to earn up to one million a year from drug research." Dr. Braithwaite goes on to cite "a number of cases where drug companies concealed and misrepresented the effects." One may also reference a Chicago Sun Times article (May 14, 2004), when the pharmaceutical company Pfizer made national news when they pled guilty to charges that a company it acquired four years prior bribed doctors to promote a medication that was not approved by the FDA. Pfizer had to pay $430 million in that drug fraud case. With all of the unscrupulous practices of the pharmaceutical industry it is no wonder that so many drugs are recalled.

The pharmaceutical drug racket is a multi-trillion dollar industry, plagued with bribery, corruption and fraud. The pharmaceutical companies have the worst record of law breaking of any other industry. So America, again I ask: When one congers up notions of drug dealers, who does one think of: Scarface, Pablo Escobar, the Mafia, Frank Lucas, the pharmaceutical companies? Is the association ludicrous? Does one see the parallel? It's all about business and profit, and the first one is always free!

America, we are a symptom driven society. Doctors and pharmaceutical companies profit by treating these symptoms. The plain and simple fact is that if we stop and take care of our spirit and our physical vessel by praying to the "God" of our understanding, get plenty of sleep, develop healthier eating habits: eat to live and not live to eat, exercise and remain active, utilize healthy support systems, and develop effective strategies to deal with life on life terms, there will be less need for all of those prescription medications. In addition, the next time you are at home and you hear one of those commercials promoting a new drug, or the next time you are at a doctor's office, flipping through a magazine to an advertisement for a new medication, or the next time you are given a free sample, take the time to read the side effects. Not too many doctors will inform you about the side effects of certain medications. Remember, the pharmaceutical companies will continue to market potentially dangerous drugs to you. Also keep in mind that one of the most lucrative times for pharmaceutical industries is when a new drug is marketed. Thought: Pharmaceutical giant, Sanofi Aventis, the forth largest in the world that makes Plavix and Ambien, made 29.3 billion in sales in 2009. Um!

CHAPTER 8: THE TOBACCO INDUSTRY

Black Top, Blue Magic, Newports: $5.00

This is not a game. What is more cunning and insidious than the alcohol or pharmaceutical industry? Hands down, it's the tobacco industry and the ravage and devastation that are left in its path. According to the U.S. Center for Disease Control, "Each year smoking kills more Americans than alcohol, cocaine, crack, heroin, homicide, suicide, automobile accidents, fires and Aids combined." In addition, "Victims die more than twenty years before the life expectancy of non smokers." According to <u>World Health</u>, "Tobacco kills more than two and a half million people prematurely every year." One must really begin to look beyond the "crack heads" and "dope fiends" and acknowledge, address, and develop resolutions for the severity of so many of the societal ills which plague America.

In the tobacco industry, who are these corporate giants? Their identity and magnitude is often convoluted in a maze of maniacal inter-relationships where one is unaware of the reign of sovereignty from one company to another. Philip Morris leads the market with 2009 assets of 9.4 billion dollars. Few people are aware, however, that the company Altria is the parent company of Phillip Morris. Specifically, Phillip Morris is the wholly owned subsidiary of the Altria Group, Inc. They sell approximately half of the 500 billion cigarettes sold in America. Phillip Morris cigarette brands include America's favorite, Marlboro and other best selling brands including Virginia Slims, Parliament, and Basic. Other brands in their portfolio include Alpine, Benson and Hedges, Bristol, Chesterfield, just to name a few. Interestingly, the tobacco company, Phillip Morris, also owns Kraft Foods, the largest confectionary food and beverage corporation in America. R J Reynolds of Winston Salem, North Carolina, is the second largest tobacco company in America. Familiar brands in their portfolio include, but are not limited to, Doral, Camel, Kool, Lucky Strike; leading cigarettes from yester-year.

The third tobacco giant is Lorillard Inc., a tobacco company owned by Loews Corporation. They are responsible for Newport, the largest selling menthol cigarette in America. Lorillard Inc. also manufacturers Kent, True, Old Gold, Maverick, Max, and Satin.

The forth tobacco giant is the Liggett Vector Brands which is the sales, marketing and distribution agent for Liggett Group and Vector Liggett Tobacco. Interestingly, the Vector Group is also highly involved in real estate in New York and California. There are also many smaller tobacco companies which also play a hand in the business called profit at the expense of the health and welfare of Americans.

Advertising

I am saddened by the ploys of big business and the reality of the profit motive which leads to such unscrupulous measures to capture and allure unsuspecting victims into their web of deceit. Once again, the power of advertising rears its ugly head to a captive audience.

One could not have lived through the 20th century and not be familiar with the Marlboro Man. Conceived in 1954 by Leo Burnett for Phillip Morris, it has been referred to as, "One of the most brilliant campaigns of all times." The imagery of a rugged cowboy, a man's man, against the backdrop of Marlboro country increased profit from 5 billion dollars in 1955 to 20 billion dollars in 1957. As recently stated, the Marlboro brand continues to be America's top selling brand. Ironically, that depiction of brute masculinity represented a brand that was originally introduced as a women's cigarette in 1924. As new information emerged in relation to the hazards of smoking, technology produced a filtered cigarette, and in 1949, the Marlboro Man became an American icon and was depicted in <u>Life Magazine</u> by Parrell Winfield. Following a 20 year stint, Winfield was replaced by Brad Johnson, a former rodeo cowboy in the 80's. Many other less popular men would also depict that rugged cowboy including Wayne Mc Laren, David Mc Lean, and Dick Hammer, all who, ironically, died from cancer.

One may also remember Virginia Slims, "You've come a long way baby." This brand was introduced in 1968 and was marketed to young professional women. One must consider the times: The 60's, feminism, women's revolution, their fight for rights and independence. In response, the tobacco industry, specifically Phillip Morris, offered women an alternative cigarette, designed by Walter Landor. The cigarette was white with a long stripe running down one side. It was longer, sleeker and more elegant and sexy in appearance. In the 90's other popular slogans were, "It's a woman's thing," and "Find your voice." I must admit that when I started smoking at the age of fourteen for all of a minute, it was because of the allure of that campaign. The Virginia Slims campaign was so popular, other industry competitors introduced their own gender specific cigarette. Specifically, the American Tobacco Company offered America Misty, Brown & Williamson gave us Capri, Liggetts introduced Eve, and R J Reynolds created Dawn.

Who does not remember Joe Camel. Of course, that is part of the problem. Even young children were enamored by this little mascot that wore sunglasses and was the ultimate cool. Joe Camel was actually created in Europe, in 1974, by a British artist for a French advertising campaign. In 1988 he was adapted by Tyron Advertising for R J Reynolds' 75th anniversary. From the end of 1987 to 1997, Joe Camel was aggressively advertised through all media venues including TV, bill boards and in every print ad one opened. Joe Camel reigned king until he came under fire in the late 90's for aversive advertising to minors.

The tobacco industry has also extended its influence on America through movies and television shows. There is a long history of collaboration between the tobacco industry and the movie industry. Think about it: Baby boomers may remember the old black and white movies from the 30's and

40's. "Between 1927 and 1951, at least 195 Hollywood stars joined cigarette ad campaigns." Reportedly, "In 1937-8 alone tobacco companies agreed to pay stars at least 3.2 million (2008 dollars) for advertising services. The tobacco company spent more to advertise Hollywood than Hollywood spent to advertise itself." WWW.Smokefreemovies.UCSF.edu/Problem/ Hollywood-Big, Tobacco Secret History in Hollywood).

Claudette Colbert, Joan Crawford, Bette Davis and Gary Cooper all plugged Lucky Strike cigarettes. Joan Crawford also plugged Old Gold, Raleigh and Chesterfield. Other actors include Barbara Stanwyck, Edward G. Robinson, Katherine Hepburn, Spencer Tracy, John Wayne, Humphrey Bogart, and Lauren Bacall. The list is endless. America was captured by their grace and style and enamored by their action and mystery. With a captive audience, the tobacco industry brokered lucrative contracts with many of these actors and Hollywood to depict smoking as sexy and alluring. In the 50's and 60's, the tobacco industry was a leading owner and sponsor of network television shows. Like pharmaceutical companies and their drugs, one could hardly watch their favorite shows without being inundated by television commercials and advertisements promoting smoking. For our younger readers, in the 70's when tobacco companies were prohibited from advertising on television and radio, the tobacco industry infused their propaganda through Hollywood films, some of which had no restrictions for minor children. What's cooler than your favorite characters or rock stars smoking cigarettes? Consider the following research conducted by the Dartmouth Medical School, Dept of Pediatrics which documents the negative impact that smoking in movies has on our young children. "The more smoking adolescents see in movies, the more likely they are to start smoking. The effect is strongest for children of non smokers." The researchers go on to say that, "Applying these results nationwide, means 390,000 kids start to smoke every year because of the movies, 120,000 of whom will die as a result." (Sargent JD, Beach ML, Adachi-Mejia HM, Gibson JJ, Titis-Erstoff LT, Carusi CP, Swan SD, Heathorton TF, Dalton MA, Dept of Pediatrics, Dartmouth Medical School, U.S. National Library of

Medicine, National Instititute of Health, Exposure to Movie Smoking: Its Relationship to Smoking Initiation Among US Adolescents). The Marlboro Man, "You've come a long way baby," Joe Camel, the movies, television shows: Advertisements have left an indelible mark on the American psyche and have exerted a profound effect on the history of the tobacco industry which has culminated in it becoming the multi billion dollar industry it is today.

Truth Ads

America, are you confused? For many years now we have not seen any television ads or commercials promoting smoking. As a matter of fact, we have been bombarded with advertisements that aggressively warn of the consequences of smoking. Has the tobacco industry suddenly developed a conscience? America, don't be fooled. Some of these truth ads, in fact are pretty impressive. As a matter of fact, like their smoking promotion predecessors, the truth ads have been quite effective disseminating the message that smoking has serious and deadly consequences, a profoundly different message. One ad that has left a lasting impression is titled, "That could be your child." It highlights young people who say, "I smoke when I get up in the morning," "I usually smoke after dinner," "Sometimes I smoke during my nap," "I'm down to about one pack a day," "I tried to quit; I need to try again." One may also remember the man with the whole in his throat, as a result of the removal of his voice box. He tells of how he used to go swimming, but now he can't. Maybe one remembers the African American woman with missing fingers or the Caucasian girl with long hair. Half of her face is normal. The other half is covered with black tar. As she puffs on a cigarette, the ad calls upon one to consider, if the outside looks like this, consider what the inside must look like. A really hilarious one is titled, "Get Your Lung Back." In this ad, a man lights up a cigarette, and coughs his lung out on to the table. He proceeds to try to catch it as it falls on to the floor and runs out the door. That's really not funny at all. There is another commercial entititled, "Confessions of the Tobacco Companies." In this ad, children are playing basketball and suddenly, cigarettes start falling from the sky. The narrative states "We have to sell cigarettes to your children. We need ½ million new smokers a year to stay in business. We have to advertise near schools. We have to lower our prices; we have to. It's nothing personal, you understand." Another commercial titled, "True Weapons of Mass Destruction," reveals, "Everyday 3000 Americans start smoking; ½ of them will die from it. How do you like those odds?" The visual that accompanies the narrative is pedestrians getting mowed down by cars, one at a time, repeatedly. Along with these truth ads, which only represent a fraction of what's out, there are numerous anti-smoking posters. One depicts Joe Camel, hooked up to an IV, in a hospital with his glasses off. A Kool cigarette ad depicts a cool kid with a pack of Kools next to him, misspelled Fool. Several Marlboro ads show, the Marlboro Man lighting up a limp cigarette depicting impotence, the Marlboro Man's horse dead in the dessert, from second hand smoke, and the "Real Marlboro Country," depicted by people huddled around smoking and coughing.

Master Settlement Agreement

Are the tobacco companies being magnanimous or is there some maniacal plan to doop the public? If you chose option 1, sadly you are wrong. If you chose option 2, sadly you are right. Maybe one remembers when the tobacco industry had to fess up and acknowledge that they were, in fact, intentionally marketing cigarettes to teens and they were well aware of the harmful effects of nicotine. All of these aggressive advertisements warning the public against the dangers of smoking are part of a 1998, $246 billion Master Settlement Agreement, filed by the Attorney Generals of 46 states against the four major tobacco companies. They include, Brown & Williamson Tobacco, Lorillard Tobacco Company, Phillip Morris Inc, R.J. Reynolds Tobacco Company, Common Wealth Tobacco and Liggett & Myers. Liggett & Myers was released from previous settlements after selling three of its four major brands to Phillip Morris. Prior to this settlement, which took approximately four years to resolve, in July, 1997, Mississippi, followed by Florida, Texas, and Minnesota recovered approximately 35-40 billion dollars in a settlement from the tobacco industry. Briefly, according to the settlement, the following monetary amounts were to be paid out annually over a 25 year period beginning 4/15/2000: Monetary fines included: Upfront damages 12.742 Billion; Annual payments of 183.177 Billion through 2025; Strategic Contribution Fund 2008-2017 8.61 Billion; National Foundation 250 Million over 10 years; Public Education Fund at least 1.45 Billion 2000-2003; State Enforcement Fund 50 Million – one time payment; National Association of Attorneys General 1.5 Billion over 10 years.

In addition, the settlement:

1. Prohibited youth targeting advertising, marketing and promotions which banned cartoon characters, and youth orientated magazines; restricted brand name sponsorships of events with significant youth audiences; banned outdoor advertising; bannned youth access to free samples; setting minimum cigarette package size.
2. Changing corporate culture required the industry to make a commitment to reduce youth access and consumption; disbanded tobacco trade associations; restricted industry labeling; opened industry records and research to the public.

Comprehensive details of the Master Settlement Agreement can be found in the National Association of Attorney Generals, Summary of the Attorney Generals' Master Settlement Agreement, March 1999, J. Johnson Wilson, National Conference of State Legislators, Director, AFI Health Committee.

In addition to the Master Settlement Agreement, there have been numerous private wrongful death and class action suits filed against the tobacco industry.

Health Consequences: Weapons of Mass Destruction

Do you smoke? Why is the question relevant? It appears that more individuals are saying no to that question; however, even with all of the restrictions and limitations adapted by society to discourage people from smoking, far too many Americans are turning a blind eye and a deaf ear to the dangerous consequences of smoking cigarettes.

So, what's in this little filtered stick of mass destruction? There are approximately 4,000 carcinogens (cancer causing agents). The major component in the cigarette is nicotine, a colorless, odorless, highly addictive, psychoactive stimulant. One may remember that psycho- active drugs work by altering the production or mimicking neurotransmitters: Chemical substances produced in the brain that integrates bodily function. Nicotine specifically mimics the neurotransmitter acetylcholine, a chemical which affects blood pressure, heart rate, memory, sleep, sexual function, just to name a few. Nicotine also increases the production of adrenaline which gives one a boost, norepinephrine, which controls arousal and alertness, and dopamine, which gives one a feeling of euphoria and pleasure. It is nicotine's effect on dopamine which makes smoking more than just "a dirty little habit." The addictive properties increase tolerance and reinforce one's desire to continue smoking, not only for pleasure, but to avoid the uncomfortable withdrawal which may include, but are not limited to, headaches, irritability, nausea, sleep disturbances, and fatigue. Given the severity of the health contradictions, it is a travesty that the tobacco companies had not acknowledged the addictive nature of nicotine until they were called out and held accountable in the Master Settlement Agreement of 1998. One may be interested in the fact that nicotine is also a common herbicide and insecticide which is used in pesticides.

Tar, a byproduct of burning tobacco, is another major ingredient in the cigarette. When one smokes, tar, a yellowish/brown sticky substance remains on the lungs and damages them. Tar is a carcinogenic and includes hydrocarbons called polycyclic aromatic hydrocarbons; including benzopyrene which has specifically been linked to lung cancer. Other components included in the cigarette which one may or may not be familiar with are: acetone which is a solvent, ammonia, a detergent, arsenic, a lethal poison, cadmium used in batteries, carbon monoxide a poisoness gas, cyanhydric acid which is used in gas chambers, DDT an insecticide, formaldehyde, and other chemicals besides the various flavoring additives.

As previously stated, the benzopyrene in tar is a leading carcinogenic. It destroys bronchial tissue and mutates genes consequently causing lung cancer, which leads in cancer deaths in America. Cancerous cells and tumors dominate the lungs, compromising functioning. In addition, smokers are more likely to experience pulmonary and bronchial obstructive lung disease. In addition to these respiratory disorders, smokers experience cardiovascular disease from plaque formation and hardening of the arteries which restrict blood flow, which can lead to strokes as well as cancer of the mouth, pancreas, bladder, and cervix.

Expectant mothers who smoke severely compromise their unborn child. The carbon monoxide and nicotine contained in cigarettes limit the amount of oxygen carried to the fetus. Babies may experience lower birth weight, upper respiratory problems and other genetic disorders. The risk of spontaneous abortion is also greatly increased.

One must also consider the mental and psychological effects that accompany smoking including depression and anxiety which is often associated with the withdrawal process.

Smokeless Tobacco

Although there is a substantial advantage to one's lungs by not smoking tobacco, smokeless tobacco including chewing tobacco and snuff pose serious health risks and are equally as addictive. Perhaps one has seen baseball players on the field with wads of dark substances in between their gums and their cheek or lower lip, with periodic dark substances being excreted from their mouth. The substance is called snuff, a mixture of dried tobacco leaves that come in a variety of flavors and scents. To date, the NCAA has banned the practice. One may still see, however, the occasional trajectory of gook from the mouth at some baseball games. Smokeless tobacco is also prevalent in certain ethnic groups, geographical locations and it has become increasingly popular among teenagers and college students. Smokeless tobacco can also lead to nicotine drug dependence. It also deteriorates the teeth, irritates the mouth and gums and digestive tract, and increases the risk of cancer of the mouth, pharynx and esophagus.

Second Hand Smoke/Third Hand Smoke

Second hand smoke, the smoke which people around smokers inhale, is also a significant cancer causing agent. Although the victim ingest less nicotine, the fumes from the burning cigarette has very high concentrations of tar. Furthermore, because one does not have the benefit of the limited protection of the filter, some of the toxins inhaled by the passive smoker are actually more carcinogenic. Newly identified is third hand smoke. Visualize a beautiful healthy baby lying on a smoker's bed, the couch, or in their parents arms. The baby breathes in fumes from the residue of the smoker. The third hand smoke can also be toxic for the baby.

America Wake Up: The Conspiracy is in the Profit Motive: The Consequences are in One's Choices

The tobacco industry can be proud of themselves. They launched one of the most aggressive advertising campaigns in history. They insidiously indoctrinated our men with promises of "machismo," our women with promises of liberation, and our children with promises of being Cool - all in the act of smoking. Their expenditures on advertising paled in relation to the billions of dollars they earned in profit. They maniacally rose above legal litigation launched by individual entities as well as Surgeon Generals of States with monetary fines, advertising restrictions and impressive truth ads that were so powerful, America was almost deceived by their true ulterior motive. How do they live with the statistics that indicate that their product kills more than alcohol, cocaine, heroin, homicide, suicide, automobile accidents, fires, and Aids combined? Has their attitude been altered by the reality of all that has happened or are these statistics just collateral damage in a game of big business and profit? In a report, "A Broken Promise to our Children," the 1998 State Tobacco Settlement 11 Years Later, issued by The Campaign for Tobacco-Free Kids, American Heart Association, American Cancer Society Action Network, American Lung Association, and Robert Wood Johnson Foundation, it is indicated that,

> Since the 1998 multi-state tobacco settlement, fines that the states are collecting record amounts of tobacco revenue, $25.1 billion this year alone-but are spending less of it on programs to prevent kids from smoking and help smokers quit. In fact, funding for tobacco prevention programs have been cut by more than 15% in the past year. (December 9, 2009)

In addition, according to a report issued by the National Survey on Drug Use and Health, (November 19, 2009), the use of menthol cigarettes which gives the sensation of coolness in the mouth and masks the harshness of cigarette smoke which had been commonly used among Blacks and other minorities, has become more popular among adolescents. Reportedly, "The rate of smoking menthol cigarettes increased from 31.0 percent in 2004 to 33.9 percent in 2008; increases were most pronounced for adolescent use, ages 12-17 (43.5 percent in 2004 vs 47.7 percent in 2008), young adults ages 18-25 (34.1 vs 40.8 percent), and males (26.9 vs 30.8 percent). America, at what point do we take responsibility?

Despite the tobacco industry's continuing profits, however, just as in the case of the alcohol and pharmaceutical industry, America can no more blame them than itself. It all always comes back to our attitude and the consequences of the choices we make. Just as with other drugs and other behaviors, the problem is not in the cigarette but in the attitude of a society which dwells in the bowels of denial, which allows one to always point the finger at someone or something else. One remembers "crack heads" and "dope fiends?" Americans continue to seek external solutions to internal problems. How did one come to believe that a little thing called a cigarette could make one something that one is not and make one feel something that is not real?

Many of us are getting the message as evidenced by the decline in cigarettes over the last twenty years, particularly among adults. But for every adult who stops smoking, thousands of children and adolescents start smoking for the first time. The promises of emancipation, being free, being an adult, "monkey see, monkey do," the feelings of affirmation, stimulation, confidence, tension reduction, and the false sense of control is a fact and an illusion for so many of our young. One starts to smoke and, by the very nature of cigarettes, that nasty little habit progresses into full blown psychological and physiological addiction. Another victim: Another dollar: Tobacco industry and all who profit from them: Shame on you.

CHAPTER 9: ENERGY DRINKS

"COCAINE": "I Love Blow": The genius of advertising. What does that say about us, America? And you thought "crack heads" and "dope fiends" were the problem!

Redux Beverages, I Love Blow: Shame on you! What were you thinking?

Just when you thought we had reached to the bottom of the barrel with Jamey Kirby's "Cocaine," following in his footsteps was Logan Gola's, "I Love Blow" energy drink. "Blow", an alias for cocaine, if possible, is even a more blatantly glamorized drug. It was marketed in vials complete with a fake mirror and a fake credit card. If one is unaware of the significance, crack cocaine users often purchase crack in vials and sniffers of cocaine customarily pour the powdery substance on to a mirror and proceed to chop it up with a credit card in order to expedite the snorting process. Even more despicable, "Blow" made available three products that sensationalized the progressive nature of the disease of addiction. Specifically, the consumer could buy, "The Stash Box Sampler Pack," including two vials of "Blow" energy drink, "The Recreational User Pack," including 24 vials of "Blow" energy drink or the "Fiender's Hook-up," including 96 vials of "Blow" energy drink. Adding further insult to injury, the product was mailed in a white, styrofoam box emulating a "brick of cocaine" (common distribution weight). The box was adorned with a scorpion and visuals of a substance that looked like cocaine. If one contacted the company, they could leave a message with an adult porn star whose voice was slurred, sounding very much like someone under the influence of cocaine. "Blow" founder, Logan Gola, has referenced his product as a sexy, edgy, alternative to Red Bull and Monster, other popular energy drinks. He further claims that he is marketing his product to an, "ultra hip party crowd and he is spoofing a life style from the 80's."

Cocaine addiction is a societal ill that influences one's quality of life and potentially destroys individuals and families. Furthermore, crack cocaine, in the 80's, devastated our communities, ravishing men and women of their souls, leaving children without parents – children who continue to struggle with emotional and learning difficulties as a result of being born from crack addicted parents. If one escaped the crack epidemic, from the crack house to the country club, individuals suffered and continue to suffer from the disease of cocaine addiction. And one dares to glamorize cocaine with marketing strategies which mimic the drug and the process of abusing it? What fuels this sick and demented thinking? Oh! That's right: It's all about profit: The energy drink industry is a multi billion dollar enterprise after all.

America, has it occurred to you that the manufacturers market their product under such provocative names because they know that it is alluring to a large population, many of whom are young? What does that say about us? Aren't you just the least bit concerned about our children and how they think? Surely, the innuendoes and glamorization of a drug today will become part of a collective consciousness and be internalized in one's psyche and wreak serious consequences tomorrow? Addiction is rooted in the attitude of a society at dis-ease. Who are more vulnerable than our young, who have not even had an opportunity to develop a healthy relationship with self, void of any mind altering substances: a little discerning, to say the least.

What about this society at dis-ease which truly believes that it can not function without a mind altering substance? Energy drinks have risen as a formidable player in the soft drink industry. One can hardly go into the neighborhood convenience store or supermarket without being inundated with an endless assortment of energy drinks with really catchy names and slogans vying for the customer's attention: "Cocaine" boast, "Speed In a Can," "Cocaine Instant Rush." "ROCKSTAR," another popular energy drink advertises their product as, "Bigger, better, faster, stronger, the world's most powerful energy drink." Who are these consumers that they target? Reportedly, the target population may be over eighteen, but the reality is that the actual consumers are young adolescents and college students. According to research firm, Mintel, in an article written by Sherri Ly at Fox News, "Last year 35% of teens regularly consumed energy drinks," which reportedly was "almost double the number five years earlier." There is also grave cause for alarm due to the reality that younger patrons, under the age of 12 are consuming far more in excess of the 80 milligrams of caffiene that are recommended for that population on a daily basis.

If you are one who has never had an energy drink, you are probably a lot more familiar with them than you think. Although original energy drinks date back over one hundred years ago in Europe and Asia, the very popular Gatorade, was originally marketed in the 60's to the University of Florida football team, the Gators, in order to replace fluids lost during strenuous activities and maintain performance. One may notice the evolution of Gatorade from Gators. In all fairness, Gatorade has maintained its' integrity and it is classified as a sports drink in contrast to an energy drink. Sports drinks generally contain less sugar and the inclusion of electrolytes which are needed salts, an aid in replenishing the water and energy which are normally lost under rigorous sports activities. It is important to note, however, that Gatorade has since developed a whole new generation of energy drinks called the G Series in order to keep up with the demands of their consumers. The G Series includes, Rehydrate & Rebuild, Hydration Muscle, and Recovery Energy.

One may also be very familiar with the energy drink Red Bull marketed in 1997 by Dietrich Mateschitz, a business man from Austria. Red Bull has cornered the American market and remains reigning king of energy drinks. To date, there are over 2000 energy drinks manufactured around the world - 300 of which are marketed in the U.S., second to China, in production followed by, but not limited to, Thailand, Germany, United Kingdom, Austria and Poland.

Target Market/Allure of Energy Drinks

Energy drinks are marketed to young consumers who want to stay awake, are too tired, or to those who are driven to keep going in order to meet the demands of daily living. This increased efficiency, along with the stimulating effects and sense of well being reinforce the allure of the product. The additional vitamins found in some energy drinks are equally appealing as is herbal additives which people often associate with good health. One may have also noticed the "5 Hour Energy craze," that cute little two ounce supplement in the blue, orange and red can that boast no sugar, no jittery feelings and no crash. In an article by Hiran Ratnayake in the Delaware New Journal (August 24, 2010), it was reported that, "5- Hour Energy brought in $320 million in wholesale revenue last year for manufacturer, Living Essentials." Ratnayake further reports that, "By the end of this year, the company projects wholesale revenues to be about 500 million."

Active Ingredient

The active ingredient in energy drinks is caffeine. Caffeine is an addictive stimulant which speeds up the central nervous system similarly but to a less degree than cocaine and amphetamines. It is the most widely used drug contained in substances such as coffee, tea, and chocolate. Caffeine is also an active ingredient in over-the-counter pain relievers such as Anacin and Excedrin and it is also contained in many of the "stay awake" medications discussed in the chapter on prescription drugs. In low doses, for some adults, there may be some beneficial properties in caffeine and it can in fact boost performance. In excess, there is potential danger which will be addressed momentarily. In addition to caffeine, other popular agents in energy drinks include taurine, an amino acid which is found naturally in the body, guarana, a South American seed which naturally contains caffeine, vitamin B6 and B12, which converts food into energy, thereby improving endurance and performance, acai, a purple berry from the Brazilian rain forest, known for its nutrient and anti-oxidative properties, ginseng, a natural stimulant, dextrose, a simple sugar and other extraneous substances.

Energy drinks initially can effect a general improvement in one's mental and cognitive functioning because of their ingredients. Americans, because of the obsessive compulsive individuals they are, over indulge. The attitude is "more," so we continue to seek out energy drinks with the highest content of caffeine and then we drink them obsessively. It is not unlikely to see individuals at bus stops or on trains in the morning starting their day with a can of Red Bull or anyone of their other favorite energy drinks. Unfortunately, the consumption of the beverage continues through out the day; many times it replaces important meals, as users are driven by time constraints and deadlines. Excessive amounts of caffeine have a profound effect on the overall functioning of the body. Although the effects vary from one individual to the next, one can suffer from caffeine intoxification or a condition called caffeinism. Consequently, one may experience restlessness, sleeplessness, heart palpitations and heart arrhythmias, anxiety, seizures, and gastrointestinal problems just to name a few. Sleep deprivation can also culminate into a full psychosis. One may consider an article written by Gary Wenk, Ph.D in Psychology Today. Reportedly, "A Kentucky man is being charged with strangling his wife with an extension cord; he claims temporary insanity triggered by excessive caffeine from diet pills, sodas and energy drinks. His defense hired a psychologist to explain how a brief psychotic disorder could be triggered by a lack of sleep." "Your Brain on Food," September 21, 2010. An excessive dose of caffeine, in fact, can also be fatal. There are also many Americans who develop a psychological and physical dependence to caffeine.

Case in point: Consider the behavior and mood of a co-worker who has not had their routinely scheduled energy drink. They may be very uncooperative, rude and less than forthcoming. Now observe them following their consumption of the energy drink. Is it the same person, one may ask: Seems not? One may notice significant changes in mood and behavior. More than likely the person is less anxious, more focused, more tolerant and more cooperative. The

Dr. Jekyll/Mr. Hyde transition is attributed to the withdrawal from caffeine, the substance which the body has developed a dependence on, in order to remain stable.

The chart below will give one an indication of the excessive amounts of caffeine contained in energy drinks in comparison to some popular beverages one may consume: Measurements are in milligrams:

Starbucks Coffee	75-330
Brewed Tea	25-110
Ice Tea	67-76
Hot Chocolate	2-25
Chocolate Milk	2-7
Cola Soda	0-54
Pain Relievers	32-65

Energy Drinks

Red Bull	80
Cocaine	280
I Love Blow	240
ROCKSTAR	160-330
Adrenalyn Shot	200
Monster	160
Super Magnum	250
5150 Juice	500
666 Energy Drink	200
All City NRG	300
Boo-Koo Energy	360
Wired X 344	344

The reality is that the labels can be inaccurate as to the percentage of caffeine in these energy drinks. Even more alarming, there is no FDA regulation on the amount of caffeine that manufacturers can include in the production of energy drinks. Where as sports drinks usually include labels with nutritional facts, sugars, calories, and other ingredients; energy drinks, classified as a natural health product are only required to list caffeine. Excessive sugar, which has no nutritional value, is also an ingredient that energy drinks omit. The combination of sugar and caffeine both of which are stimulants send our body into a spiraling incline upward followed by a descent, further perpetuating dependence which ultimately reigns harm on our health. Excessive sugar has also been linked to obesity, diabetes, tooth decay, premature aging and other degenerative disorders.

Energy Drinks and Alcohol

As Americans continue on their quest to get outside of "self," a potentially dangerous trend has developed among adolescents, college students, and young adults: Mixing energy drinks with alcohol. In an article by Bill Hendrick for WebMD Health News, Dennis Thombs, PhD, is quoted as saying that, "28% of college drinkers drink alcohol mixed with energy drinks in a typical month." Dr. Thombs goes on to relate that "The phenomenon is so common, that researchers have coined an acronym for it: AMED, for alcohol-mixed-with-energy-drinks." One may remember from the chapter on alcohol, that it is a depressant, in other words, it slows down the central nervous system. The caffeine in energy drinks classify it as a stimulant. When one mixes a stimulant with a depressant, there is a speed ball effect. The heart rate and blood pressure, for example fluctuates from a hyper-vigilant to a hypo-vigilant state: It speeds up and slows down. In addition, alcohol alters one's visual motor skills, compromises one's perception of pain and time, just to name a few consequences. When alcohol is mixed with a stimulant, these distortions are masked. Ironically, that is part of the allure of mixing energy drinks with alcohol. The combination perpetuates the illusion that the individual can party longer, and harder, but the reality is that the individual may lose track of how much alcohol they are consuming which more than likely will result in them consuming more than what is recommended in any designated period of time. In that same article by Bill Hendrick, Bruce Goldberg, Ph.D, director of toxicology at the University of Florida relates that "This condition is often described as "wide awake and drunk."' One may remember that the body can only metabolize a half ounce of alcohol within an hour. Now consider the individual who subjectively believes that they can drive home. Hopefully, one is now getting the picture. In addition, alcohol and caffeine independently and collectively dehydrate the body, which is one cause of the all too familiar hangover. An article in USA Today (10/08) reported that Roland Griffiths, a neuro-scientist at Johns Hopkins School of Medicine, "wrote a letter to the FDA calling for increased legislation of energy drinks. The petition signed by 100 scientists and physicians cited the risk to young drinkers of caffeine-intoxification and alcohol related injuries as a major concern:" So much for legislation.

It is a sad reality that some energy drink manufacturers have begun marketing energy drinks pre-mixed with alcohol. One such drink is the Four Loko Energy Drink. It contains the traditional taurine, guarana, and caffeine with 12% alcohol. According to Tony Aiello of CBS News, (August 26, 2010), "One can is equivalent to the alcohol in three beers, the caffeine of one cup of coffee and a Red Bull." It is marketed in a variety of flavors including, orange, fruit punch, grape, watermelon, blue raspberry, lemonade, cranberry lemonade and Brazillian Berry and it targets adolescence and college students. Aiello reports that a 14 year old Westchester girl got sick from the drink. Reportedly, "The caffeine buzz delayed her from feeling the effect of the alcohol." Aiello's report goes on to indicate that emergency room doctors at Lawrence Hospital are seeing more incidences of young victims of this dangerous trend. Ironically despite the dangers of premixed energy drinks and alcohol, more energy drink manufacturers are considering marketing their own version of this dangerous mix. It is even more alarming that there is a market for them. America, we have a problem.

Note: Pageant moms and "Go Go Juice," a combination of Mountain Dew and Red Bull: Stop it! You are jeopardizing the health and well being of your child, and for what? Their fame or yours? Your actions are a precursor to future addictions. Remember, it's all about the attitude!

Note: "Cocaine"

The FDA issued a warning that said, "Redux was illegally marketing the drink as a street drug alternative and a dietary supplement." Shortly there after, they remarketed the drink under the name, "No Name." As of to date, the product has resumed its' original name, "Cocaine". In addition, one may buy "Cocaine Cut," now recognized in the blue can in a milder version without the burn and "Cocaine Free," with no sugar. It is available on store shelves, web sites and individuals continue to order the product: So much for accountability!

Note: "I Love Blow"

The FDA did warn of taking legal action against the product. It was advertised on the Web and on My Space which is one of the largest social networking sites geared to our young. Although one can continue to access information on the product, reportedly, it is no longer available to order on the website. The availability of the product is currently being determined.

CHAPTER 10: OXYGEN BARS

Remember: It's the Attitude

Oxygen 99% Pure		*Kids Lose It. Adults Need It*
Breathe and Believe	***Advertisements***	*Oxygen with Infused Oils*
		Menthol or Grapefruit
Oxygen: Party Bar Rentals	*We Serve Fun*	*Oxygen In a Can*

Oxygen: The most vital element to life, health and well being. We breathe in oxygen: It is infused with hemoglobin in our blood and distributed throughout every cell in the body. With Americans' obsession with getting outside of themselves, it is not surprising that we continue to line up at oxygen bars around the country to inhale pure oxygen through a plastic hose called canola which is inserted directly into the nostrils. And if that is not enough, the option to infuse essential oils such as lavender, ecliptic, peppermint, and cranberry, flavor the oxygen as it penetrates the lungs by breathing in through the nose and out through the mouth. The experience promises supreme relaxation, relief of stress and tensions, increased memory retention, reduction in insomnia, reduction in headaches, opens sinuses, minimization of hangovers and an overall feeling of energy and well being. The cost is approximately one dollar per minute and generally customers, of course, depending on their finances will go the max of 20 minutes.

Oxygen bars is a trend that gained prominence in the United States in the 90's and has maintained popularity targeting of course teens who promote it at parties and advertise it as fun and to adults looking for a quick fix. The opening of actor, Woody Harrelson's O2 Oxygen Bar, which opened on Sunset Strip, in California in 1998, was one of the hottest night clubs on the strip at that time. It was caffeine and alcohol free and advertised as an "alternative bar experience." Patrons comfortably sat on big cushions and breathed in oxygen through breathing tubes connected to hookah pipes for $13 a hit.

The practice of inhaling pure oxygen started in Tokyo and Beijing in the early 90's. It was their solution to a dense population and polluted air from industry which had potentially damaging effects on their lungs. A significant difference, however, is that Japan's oxygen bars were not used recreationally in bars and at parties. They were used in clinics and offices in the day time with the express purpose of providing much needed clean air. Interestingly, some of the wealthier Japanese had mini oxygen generators as a staple in their homes. They compared it to; the best thing since bottled water. From Asia, it spread into Canada and then to California, Las Vegas and then to New York. Oxygen bars can now be found in airports, nightclubs, health clubs, resorts, tanning salons and casinos just to name a few. Casinos, for example, spend hundreds of thousands of dollars on an oxygen infiltration system which pumps in pure oxygen to keep its' patrons up, and alert and gambling over long periods of time, which of course is lucrative for business.

What's That All About?

Well, so what is all the fuss about? How could inhaling a very natural substance with clear benefits hurt? You see, the problem is not so much what we are doing, but why we are doing it. Remember, just like drugs, drugs in and of themselves are not bad. Thank God, we live in a technologically advanced society where drugs are available to enhance the quality of life and even saves lives. So, it's not the drug, it's not the oxygen, it's the attitude. Its how we think, it's our relationship to it. It's our overwhelming need to escape to a higher plane: To nirvana. Rather than developing the tools and strategies to help ourselves live life on life terms, we run to that better place, or what we think is a better place. We succumb to the notion that we don't have to fight the fight, we don't have to rely on our inner strength, we don't have to rely on our sense of spirituality. We mistakenly believe that the solution to all of our problems is always in getting high. What did the song say, "Higher?"

Oxygen: We are inclined to take something so basic and turn it into an obsession which says a lot about who we are and how we think. And don't be fooled, America. Don't naively think that it is just oxygen and no one is stealing and killing for it. The euphoria we achieve from all mind altering substances, the buzz from the glass of wine, the Grey Goose, the Tequila, the well being from the joint, the power from the lines of coke and the ability of heroin to lull one into a place where the sharp edges of reality disappear is the same drive as the compulsive trend to pay $10 for pure oxygen.

Side Effects

And what about the side effects of this little trend we have going on? Our bodies operate in a state of equilibrium, which means that there has to be a perfect balance of the elements that are introduced into the body. The normal atmospheric content of oxygen in the air is 21%. The percentage of oxygen one breaths in at oxygen bars can be as high as 99%. In addition, the oxygen used in oxygen bars is not necessarily medical gas. It is ambient oxygen which is industrial in nature. Although oxygen therapy has proven to have medicinal properties some medical professionals warn that individuals with certain respiratory disorders should not inhale too much oxygen. Ultimately, too much oxygen can be toxic.

America: "A drug is a drug," and any substance which alters the brain chemistry and physiological function of the body is a drug. The federal government, does in fact, regulate oxygen as a drug, so don't minimize it. It is our maladaptive way of dealing with life. As long as we minimize our need to get outside ourselves with any substance, we remain in bondage and susceptible to using and abusing other substances which can have deadly consequences. So we have to get honest. The trend in oxygen bars is potentially dangerous because it condones irresponsibility and minimizes self efficacy, particularly for our youth. We have to stop looking for easy ways out. We must hold ourselves accountable and not let the immediate gratification of a quick high navigate our ship. The drug epidemic is not our problem. The way we think is our problem. America, hold yourself accountable. America: Get honest!

EPILOGUE: LOST SOULS RECLAIMED

The little child: The child within

Who are these children with eyes so wide and smile so broad

We look at them, but we do not see

We hear them, but we do not listen

What is it that has the power of a nuclear weapon: The destruction of an atom bomb

It is the insanity of life

Words that cut bearing forth invisible blood

Violations that permeate the essence of our soul: Our very being

Pain so great we are crippled in our escape

To a place that transcends the here and now

A place which severs the ties of reality

A place of solace and serenity

A place born from the destruction and devastation of our lives

A small hand extends from behind the barrier

Little eyes peeking out to see if it is safe to return: But it's not

The insanity lurks bigger as ever

Waiting to consume the soul

We retreat: Over and over again

Until we lose our way home

What happened to that child

They have ascended to that place of total alienation

Alienation from the world but connected to some force unknown

That child so lost: listen to their cries

I cut myself so I can feel

Food offers me a sense of security wrapping me in a cocoon: safe from the world I know

Heroin rushing through my veins is the only warmth I know

Cocaine makes me feel like Goliath: Ready to battle the demons

Alcohol minimizes the harsh reality of my mere existence

Relationships give me the illusion of connectedness and sex reminds me that I am in fact alive

Shopping appeases me

Gambling gives my dead soul a rush

Psychedelic drugs electrify me and bring me to life

The duplicity of the internet allows me to travel to cyber space: A place where no man has gone or the only place where I can be accepted by people just like me.

Flesh gives me a sense of power and is the total embodiment of union: All things in one

A soul lost: Joining other souls who float endlessly through the universe looking for a connection

The irony is, the very thing that brings me solace, destroys me

I am caught in the perpetual destruction of my mere existence

A glimmer of light: A familiar smell: A notable sound

Out of no where: A bolt of lightning: An unsuspecting ray of hope that warms me in a way I have never imagined

It is familiar but so strange

That power greater than me: Greater than the pain: Greater than all that is holy:

A faint voice bellowing in the wind

Words so sharp they penetrate my soul: Stop the insanity: The path has been lightened before you. Open your eyes and see: Open your ears and listen. You possess the power: recapture your soul

Your mantra will sustain you:

I am God's child

I am blessed

I can live

My past does not define me

I am destined for greater things

I choose to turn from the darkness that is here and now and forever I will walk in the footprints of my supreme being

I am created in light to live in light

I sever the bonds that consume me

I live

I reclaim my soul

I reclaim my spirit

Epilogue: The Awakening: There is no Such Thing as a "Crack Head" or a "Dope Fiend"

Condemnation of some equals the inevitable destruction of all. The disease that plagues America is minimized by the reductionist attitude that illuminates the despair of a few. America, it is now or never. We are called upon to broaden our perspective from "them" to "us." "Crack heads," "dope fiends," no: My child, your sister or brother, their aunt or uncle, our mother or father. Lost souls become lost spirits. We are all interconnected: Our spirits bind us to a power greater than ourselves.

Human attributes: Kindness, compassion, patience, tolerance: Apply them to self first: Learn to love self: Extend that love to others.

For everyone you see that is still sick and in pain, engaging in self defeating behavior, hiding behind the illusion of well being and security: Embrace them. Extend your love to them. For they are an extension of you, an extension of us and of all that is one.

CPSIA information can be obtained
at www.ICGtesting.com
Printed in the USA
BVHW032310120919
558283BV00002B/271/P